BASIC STEPS
FOR
SPIRITUAL
GROWTH

R. A. TORREY

WHITAKER
HOUSE

All Scripture quotations are taken from the King James Version of the Holy Bible.

BASIC STEPS FOR SPIRITUAL GROWTH
(Three Books in One)

ISBN: 978-1-64123-173-2
eBook ISBN: 978-1-64123-174-9
Printed in the United States of America
© 1984, 1986 by Whitaker House

Whitaker House
1030 Hunt Valley Circle
New Kensington, PA 15068
www.whitakerhouse.com

Library of Congress Cataloging-in-Publication Data
Names: Torrey, R. A. (Reuben Archer), 1856-1928, author.
Title: Basic steps for spiritual growth / by R.A. Torrey.
Description: New Kensington, PA : Whitaker House, 2019. |
Identifiers: LCCN 2018060692 (print) | LCCN 2019003683 (ebook) |
   ISBN 9781641231749 (ebook) | ISBN 9781641231732 (trade pbk. : alk. paper)
Subjects: LCSH: Spiritual formation. | Prayer—Christianity. |
   Bible—Hermeneutics. | Witness bearing (Christianity)
Classification: LCC BV4511 (ebook) | LCC BV4511 .T67 2019 (print) |
   DDC 248.4—dc23
LC record available at https://lccn.loc.gov/2018060692

2 3 4 5 6 7 8 9 10 11 **ய** 26 25 24 23 22 21 20 19

CONTENTS

HOW TO PRAY

CHAPTER 1

THE IMPORTANCE OF PRAYER

In Ephesians 6:18, the tremendous importance of prayer is expressed with startling and overwhelming force: "[Pray] *always with all prayer and supplication in the Spirit, and watching thereunto with all perseverance and supplication for all saints.*" When the perceptive child of God stops to weigh the meaning of these words, then notes the connection in which they are found; he or she is driven to say, "I must pray, pray, pray. I must put all my energy and heart into prayer. Whatever else I do, I must pray."

Notice the *alls*: "*all prayer and supplication...all perseverance...for all saints.*" Note the piling up of strong words: "*prayer*," "*supplication*," "*perseverance.*" Also notice the strong expression "*watching,*" more literally, "in this, be not lazy." Paul realized the natural apathy of man, especially his natural neglect in prayer. How seldom we pray things through! How often the church and the individual get right up to the verge of a great blessing in prayer and then let go, become lazy, and quit. I wish that the words "in this, be not lazy" might burn into our hearts. I wish that the whole verse would burn into our hearts.

THE NECESSITY OF PERSISTENT PRAYER

Why is this constant, persistent, sleepless, overcoming prayer so necessary? Because there is a devil. He is cunning; he is mighty; he never rests; he is continually plotting the downfall of the children of God. If the children of God relax in prayer, the devil will succeed in ensnaring them.

Ephesians 6:12–13 reads:

For we wrestle not against flesh and blood, but against principalities, against powers, against the rulers of the darkness of this world, against spiritual wickedness in high places. Wherefore take unto you the whole armour of God, that ye may be able to withstand in the evil day, and having done all, to stand.

7

Next follows a description of the different parts of the Christian's armor that we are to put on if we are to stand against Satan and his mighty schemes. Paul brings his message to a climax in Ephesians 6:18, telling us that to all else we must add prayer—constant, persistent, untiring, sleepless prayer in the Holy Spirit—or all will be in vain.

Prayer is God's appointed way for obtaining things. The reason we lack anything in life is due to a neglect of prayer. James pointed this out very forcibly: *"Ye have not, because ye ask not"* (James 4:2). The secret behind the poverty and powerlessness of the average Christian is neglect of prayer.

Many Christians are asking, "Why is it that I progress so little in my Christian life?"

"Neglect of prayer," God answers. "You do not have because you do not ask."

Many ministers are asking, "Why is it I see so little fruit from my labors?"

Again, God answers, "Neglect of prayer. You do not have because you do not ask."

Many Sunday-school teachers are asking, "Why is it that I see so few converted in my Sunday school class?"

Still, God answers, "Neglect of prayer. You do not have because you do not ask."

Both ministers and churches are asking, "Why is it that the church of Christ makes so little headway against unbelief, error, sin, and worldliness?"

Once more, we hear God answering, "Neglect of prayer. You do not have because you do not ask."

Those men whom God set forth as a pattern of what He expected Christians to be—the apostles—regarded prayer as the most important business of their lives. When the multiplying responsibilities of the early church crowded in upon them, this was the response of the twelve disciples:

Then the twelve called the multitude of the disciples unto them, and said, It is not reason that we should leave the word of God, and serve tables. Wherefore, brethren, look ye out among you seven men of honest report, full of the Holy Ghost and wisdom, whom we may appoint over this business. But we will give ourselves continually to prayer, and to the ministry of the word. (Acts 6:2–4)

From what Paul wrote to both churches and individuals, it is evident that much of his time, strength, and thought were devoted to prayer for them. (See Romans 1:9; Ephesians 1:15–16; Colossians 1:9; 1 Thessalonians 3:10; and 2 Timothy 1:3.) All the mighty men of God outside the Bible have been men of prayer. They have differed from one another in many things, but in this practice of faithful praying, they have been alike.

THE MINISTRY OF INTERCESSION

Prayer occupied a very prominent place and played a very important part in the earthly life of our Lord. Turn, for example, to Mark 1:35: *"And in the morning, rising up a great while before day, he went out, and departed into a solitary place, and there prayed."* The preceding day had been a very busy and exciting one, but Jesus shortened the hours of needed sleep so that He could rise early and give Himself to more sorely needed prayer.

Turn to Luke 6:12, where we read: *"It came to pass in those days, that he went out into a mountain to pray, and continued all night in prayer to God."* Our Savior occasionally found it necessary to spend a whole night in prayer.

The words *pray* and *prayer* are used at least twentyfive times in connection with our Lord in the brief record of His life in the four Gospels, and His praying is mentioned in places where these words are not used. Evidently prayer took much of Jesus' time and strength. A man or woman who does not spend much time in prayer cannot properly be called a follower of Jesus Christ.

Praying is the most important part of the present ministry of our risen Lord. This reason for constant, persistent, sleepless, overcoming prayer seems, if possible, even more forcible than the others.

Christ's ministry did not end with His death. His atoning work was finished then, but when He rose and ascended to the right hand of the Father, He entered into other work for us, work just as important in its place as His atoning work. It cannot be separated from His atonement because it rests on that as its basis and is necessary to our complete salvation.

We read what that great, present work is by which He carries our salvation on to completeness: *"Wherefore he is able also to save them to the uttermost that come unto God by him, seeing he ever liveth to make intercession for them."* (Hebrews 7:25). This verse tells us that Jesus is able to save us to the uttermost, not merely *from* the uttermost, but *to* the uttermost—to entire completeness and absolute perfection. He is able to do this not only because He died but also because He *"ever liveth."*

The verse also tells us why He now lives: *"to make intercession"*—to pray. Praying is the principal thing He is doing in these days. It is by His prayers that He is saving us.

The same thought is found in Paul's remarkable, triumphant challenge: *"Who is he that condemneth? It is Christ that died, yea rather, that is risen again, who is even at the right hand of God, who also maketh intercession for us"* (Romans 8:34).

If we are to have fellowship with Jesus Christ in His present work, we must spend much time in prayer. We must give ourselves to earnest, constant, persistent, sleepless, overcoming prayer.

I know of nothing that has so impressed me with a sense of the importance of praying at all seasons—being much and constantly in prayer—as the thought that this is the principal occupation of my risen Lord even now. I want to have fellowship with Him. For that reason, I have asked the Father, whatever else He may make me, to make me an intercessor. I pray that He will make me a man who knows how to pray and who spends much time in prayer.

This ministry of intercession is glorious and mighty, and we can all have a part in it. The man or woman who cannot attend a prayer meeting because of illness can have a part in it. The busy mother and the woman who works outside the home can have a part. They can mingle prayers for the saints, for their pastor, for the unsaved, and for missionaries with their day's work. The hard-driven man of business can have a part in it, praying as he hurries from duty to duty. But we must, if we want to maintain this spirit of constant prayer, take time—and plenty of it—when we shut ourselves up in the secret place alone with God for nothing but prayer.

RECEIVING MERCY, GRACE, AND JOY

Prayer is the means that God has appointed for our receiving mercy and obtaining grace. Hebrews 4:16 is one of the simplest, sweetest verses in the Bible: *"Let us therefore come boldly unto the throne of grace, that we may obtain mercy, and find grace to help in time of need."* These words make it very clear that God has appointed a way by which we can seek and obtain mercy and grace. That way is prayer—a bold, confident, outspoken approach to the throne of grace, the Most Holy Place of God's presence. There our sympathizing High Priest, Jesus Christ, has entered in our behalf. (See Hebrews 4:14–15.)

Mercy is what we need, and grace is what we must have; otherwise, all our lives and efforts will end in complete failure. Prayer is the way to obtain mercy and grace. Infinite grace is at our disposal, and we make it ours by prayer. It is ours for the asking. Oh, if we only realized the fullness of God's grace—its height, depth, length, and breadth—I am sure we would spend more time in prayer. The measure of our appropriation of grace is determined by the measure of our prayers.

Who does not feel that he needs more grace? Then ask for it. Be constant and persistent in your asking. Be diligent and untiring in your asking. God delights in our persistence in prayer, for it shows our faith in Him, and He is mightily pleased with faith. Because of our perseverance, He will rise and give us as much as we need. (See Luke 11:8.) What little streams of mercy and grace most of us know when we might know rivers overflowing their banks!

Prayer in the name of Jesus Christ is the way He Himself has appointed for His disciples to obtain fullness of joy. He states this simply and beautifully: *"Hitherto have ye asked nothing in my name: ask, and ye shall receive, that your joy may be full"* (John 16:24). Who does not wish for joy? Well, the way to have full joy is by praying in the name of Jesus. We all know people who are full of joy. Indeed, it is just running over, shining from their eyes, bubbling out of their very lips, and running off their fingertips when they shake your hand. Coming in contact with them is like coming in contact with an electrical machine charged with gladness. People of that sort are always people who spend much time in prayer.

Why is it that prayer in the name of Christ brings such fullness of joy? In part, because we get what we ask. But that is not the only reason, nor is it the greatest. Prayer makes God real. When we ask something definite of God, and He gives it, how real God becomes! He is right there! It is blessed to have a God who is real and not merely an idea. I remember once when I suddenly and seriously fell ill all alone in my study. I dropped on my knees and cried to God for help. Instantly, all pain left me, and I was perfectly well. It seemed as if God stood right there, reached out His hand, and touched me. The joy of the healing was not as great as the joy of meeting God.

No joy on earth or in heaven is greater than communion with God. Prayer in the name of Jesus brings us into communion with God. The psalmist was surely not speaking only of future blessedness but also of present blessedness, when he said, *"In thy presence is fulness of joy"* (Psalm 16:11). Oh, the unutterable joy of those moments when, in our prayers, we really enter into the presence of God!

Does someone say, "I have never known joy like that in prayer"? Do you take enough leisure for prayer to actually sense God's presence? Do you really give yourself up to prayer in the time that you do take?

FREEDOM FROM ANXIETY

In every care, anxiety, and need of life, prayer with thanksgiving is the means that God has appointed for our obtaining freedom from all anxiety and the peace of God that passes all understanding. Paul said,

> *Be careful for nothing; but in every thing by prayer and supplication with thanksgiving let your requests be made known unto God. And the peace of God, which passeth all understanding, shall keep your hearts and minds through Christ Jesus.*   (Philippians 4:6–7)

To many, this initially seems like the picture of a life that is beautiful but beyond the reach of ordinary mortals. This is not so at all. The verse tells us how this life of peace is attainable by every child of God: *"Be careful for nothing"* (verse 6). The remainder of the verse tells us how to do this. It is very simple: *"But in every thing by prayer and supplication with thanksgiving let your requests be made known unto God."*

What could be plainer or simpler than that? Just keep in constant touch with God. When troubles or afflictions—great or small—occur, speak to Him about it, never forgetting to return thanks for what He has already done. What will the result be? *"The peace of God, which passeth all understanding, shall keep your hearts and minds through Christ Jesus"* (verse 7).

That is glorious, and it is as simple as it is glorious! Thank God, many are trying it. Do you know anyone who is always serene? Perhaps this person has a very temperamental nature. Nevertheless, when troubles, conflicts, opposition, and sorrow sweep around him, the peace of God that is beyond all understanding will keep his heart and his thoughts in Christ Jesus.

We all know people like that. How do they do it? By prayer, that is how. They know the deep peace of God, the unfathomable peace that surpasses all understanding, because they are men and women of much prayer.

Some of us let the hurry of our lives crowd prayer out; what a waste of time, energy, and emotion there is in this constant worry! One night of prayer will save us from many nights of insomnia. Time spent in prayer is not wasted; it is time invested at a big interest.

VEHICLE FOR THE HOLY SPIRIT

Prayer is the method that God Himself has appointed for our obtaining the Holy Spirit. The Bible is very plain on this point. Jesus said, *"If ye then, being evil, know how to give good gifts unto your children: how much more shall your heavenly Father give the Holy Spirit to them that ask him?"* (Luke 11:13).

I know this as definitely as I know that my thirst is quenched when I drink water. Early one morning in the Chicago Avenue Church prayer room, where several hundred people had been assembled a number of hours in prayer, the Holy Spirit fell so fully that no one could speak or pray. The whole place was so filled with His presence that sobs of joy filled the place. Men left that room and went to different parts of the country, taking trains that very morning, and the effects of the outpouring of God's Holy Spirit in answer to prayer were soon reported. Others went into the city with the blessing of God on them. This is only one instance among many that might be cited from personal experience.

If we would only spend more time in prayer, there would be more fullness of the Spirit's power in our work. Many who once worked unmistakably in the power of the Holy Spirit now fill a room with empty shoutings, beating the air with meaningless gestures, because they have neglected prayer. We must spend much time on our knees before God if we are to continue in the power of the Holy Spirit.

BE READY FOR HIS RETURN

Prayer is the means that Christ has appointed so that our hearts will not be overcome with indulgences, drunkenness, and the cares of this life, so that the day of Christ's return will not come upon us suddenly as a snare. (See Luke 21:34–35.) We are warned in Scripture: "*Watch…therefore, and pray always, that* [we] *may be accounted worthy to escape all these things that shall come to pass, and to stand before the Son of man*" (Luke 21:36). According to this passage, there is only one way that we can be prepared for the coming of the Lord when He appears: through much prayer.

> THE WORLD TENDS TO DRAW US DOWN BY ITS SELF-INDULGENCES AND CARES. THERE IS ONLY ONE WAY BY WHICH WE CAN TRIUMPHANTLY RISE ABOVE THESE THINGS—BY CONSTANT WATCHING IN PRAYER, THAT IS, BY SLEEPLESSNESS IN PRAYER.

The second coming of Jesus Christ is a subject that is awakening much interest and discussion in our day. It is one thing to be interested in the Lord's return and to talk about it, but it is another thing to be prepared for it. We live in an atmosphere that has a constant tendency to make us unsuitable for Christ's coming. The world tends to draw us down by its self-indulgences and cares. There is only one way by which we can triumphantly rise above these things—by constant watching in prayer, that is, by sleeplessness in prayer. "*Watch*" in this passage is the same strong word used in Ephesians 6:18, and *"always"* means to pray at all times. The man who spends little time in prayer, who is not steadfast and constant in prayer, will not be ready for the Lord when He comes. But we can be ready. How? Pray! Pray! Pray!

WE NEED TO PRAY

Prayer is necessary because of what it accomplishes. Much has been said about that already, but more should be added. Prayer promotes our spiritual growth as almost nothing else, indeed, as nothing else except Bible study. Prayer and Bible study go hand in hand.

Through prayer, my sin—my most hidden sin—is brought to light. As I kneel before God and pray, *"Search me, O God, and know my heart: try me, and know my thoughts: And see if there be any wicked way in me"* (Psalm 139:23–24), God directs the penetrating rays of His light into the innermost recesses of my heart. The sins I never suspected to be present are brought to light. In answer to prayer, God washes away my iniquity and cleanses my sin. (See Psalm 51:2.) My eyes are opened to behold wondrous things out of God's Word. (See Psalm 119:18.) I receive wisdom to know God's way (see James 1:5) and strength to walk in it. As I meet God in prayer and gaze into His face, I am changed into His image *"from glory to glory"* (2 Corinthians 3:18). Each day of true prayer life finds me more like my glorious Lord.

John Welch, the son-in-law of John Knox, was one of the most faithful men of prayer this world has ever seen. He counted any day in which seven or eight hours were not devoted solely to God in prayer and the study of His Word as wasted time. An old man speaking of him after his death said, "He was a type of Christ." How did he become so like his Master? His prayer life explains the mystery.

Prayer also brings power into our work. If we wish power for any work to which God calls us, whether it is preaching, teaching, personal work, or the raising of our children, we can receive it by earnest prayer.

A woman, with a little boy who was perfectly incorrigible, once came to me in desperation and said, "What should I do with him?"

I asked, "Have you ever tried prayer?"

She said that she had prayed for him, she thought. I asked if she had made his conversion and his character a matter of specific, expectant prayer. She replied that she had not been definite in the matter. She began that day, and at once there was a marked change in the child. As a result, he grew up into Christian manhood.

How many Sunday-school teachers have taught for months and years and seen no real fruit from their labors? Then, they learn the secret of intercession; by earnest pleading with God, they see their students, one by one, brought to Christ! How many poor teachers have become mighty people of God by casting away their confidence in their own abilities and gifts and giving themselves up to God to wait on Him for the *"power from on high"* (Luke 24:49)! Along with other believers, the Scottish evangelist John Livingstone spent a night in prayer to God. When he preached the next day, five hundred people were either converted or marked some definite uplift in their spiritual lives. Prayer and power are inseparable.

Prayer avails for the conversion of others. Few people are converted in this world in any other way than in connection with someone's prayers. I previously thought that no human being had anything to do with my own conversion, for I was not converted in church or Sunday school or in personal conversation with anyone. I was awakened in the middle of the night and converted. As far as I can remember, I did not have the slightest thought of being converted, or of anything of that nature, when I went to bed and fell asleep. But I was awakened in the middle of the night and converted probably within five minutes. A few minutes before, I was about as near eternal damnation as one gets. I had one foot over the brink and was trying to get the other one over. As I said, I thought no human being had anything to do with it, but I had forgotten my mother's prayers. Later, I learned that one of my college classmates had decided to pray for me until I was saved.

Prayer often avails where everything else fails. How utterly all of Monica's efforts and entreaties failed with her son! But her prayers prevailed with God, and the immoral youth became St. Augustine, the mighty man of God. By prayer, the bitterest enemies of the gospel have become its most valiant defenders, the most wicked the truest sons of God, and the most contemptible women the purest saints. Oh, the power of prayer to reach down, where hope itself seems vain, and lift men and women up into fellowship with and likeness to God! It is simply wonderful! How little we appreciate this marvelous weapon!

> BY PRAYER, THE BITTEREST ENEMIES OF THE GOSPEL HAVE BECOME ITS MOST VALIANT DEFENDERS, THE MOST WICKED THE TRUEST SONS OF GOD, AND THE MOST CONTEMPTIBLE WOMEN THE PUREST SAINTS.

Prayer brings blessings to the church. The history of the church has always been full of grave difficulties to overcome. The devil hates the church and seeks in every way to block its progress by false doctrine, by division, and by inward corruption of life. But by prayer, a clear way can be made through everything. Prayer will root out heresy, smooth out misunderstanding, sweep away jealousies and animosities, obliterate immoralities, and bring in the full tide of God's reviving grace. History abundantly proves this. In the darkest hour, when the state of the church has seemed beyond hope, believing men and women have met together and cried to God, and the answer has come.

It was so in the days of Knox and in the days of Wesley, Whitefield, Edwards, and Brainerd. It was so in the days of Finney and in the days of the great revival of 1857 in this country and of 1859 in Ireland. And it will be so again in your day and mine! Satan has organized his forces. Some people, claiming great apostolic methods, are merely covering the rankest dishonesty and hypocrisy with their loud and false assurance. Christians equally loyal to the great fundamental truths of the gospel are scowling at one another with a devilsent suspicion. The world, the flesh, and the devil are holding a merry carnival. It is a dark day, but now *"it is time for thee, Lord, to work: for they have made void thy law"* (Psalm 119:126). He is getting ready to work, and now He is listening for the voice of prayer. Will He hear it? Will He hear it from you? Will He hear it from the church as a body? I believe He will.

CHAPTER 2

PRAYING TO GOD

After having seen some of the tremendous importance and irresistible power of prayer, we now come directly to the lesson—how to pray with power.

In the Acts 12, we have the record of a prayer that prevailed with God and also brought about great results. In the fifth verse of this chapter, the manner and method of this prayer are described in a few words: *"Prayer was made without ceasing of the church unto God for him"* (Acts 12:5). The first thing to notice in this verse is the brief expression *"unto God."* The prayer that has power is the prayer that is offered to God.

But some will say, "Is not all prayer offered to God?" No. Much of so-called prayer, both public and private, is not directed to God. In order for a prayer to really be to God, there must be a definite and conscious approach to Him when we pray. We must have an explicit and vivid realization that He is bending over us and listening as we pray. In too many of our prayers, God is thought of too little. Our minds are taken up with thoughts of what we need and are not occupied with thoughts of the mighty and loving Father from whom we are seeking our requests. Often, we are neither occupied with the need nor with the One to whom we are praying. Instead, our minds are wandering here and there. There is no power in that sort of prayer. But when we really come into God's presence, really meet Him face-to-face in the place of prayer, really seek the things that we desire from Him, then there is power.

COMING INTO GOD'S PRESENCE

If we want to pray correctly, the first thing we should do is to make sure that we really seek an audience with God—that we really come into His very presence. Before a word of petition is offered, we should have the definite and vivid consciousness that we are talking to God. Also, we should believe that He is listening to our requests and is going to grant the things that we ask of Him. This is only possible by the Holy Spirit's power, so we should look to the Holy Spirit to lead us into the presence of God. And we should not be hasty in words until He has actually brought us there.

One night, a very active Christian man dropped into a prayer meeting that I was leading. Before we knelt to pray, I said something like the above, telling all the friends to be sure that before they prayed, they were really in God's presence. I also explained that while they were praying, they should have thoughts of God definitely in mind and be more taken up with Him than with their petitions. A few days later, I met this same gentleman. He said that this simple thought was entirely new to him. It had made prayer a completely new experience for him. If we want to pray correctly, these two little words must sink deep into our hearts: "*unto God.*"

PRAY WITHOUT CEASING

The second secret of effective praying is found in the same verse in the words "*prayer...without ceasing.*" The words "*without ceasing*" do not convey the full force of the original Greek. The word literally means "stretched-out-ed-ly." It is a pictorial word and wonderfully expressive. It represents the soul on a stretch of earnest and intense desire. *Intensely* would perhaps be as close a translation as any English word. It is the same word used to speak of our Lord in Luke 22:44, where it is said, "*And being in an agony he prayed more earnestly: and his sweat was as it were great drops of blood falling down to the ground.*"

We read in Hebrews 5:7 that Christ "*in the days of his flesh...offered up prayers and supplications with strong crying and tears.*" In Romans 15:30, Paul begged the saints in Rome to "*strive together*" with him in their prayers. The word translated "*strive*" means primarily to contend as in athletic games or in a fight. In other words, prayer that prevails with God is prayer into which we put our whole souls, stretching out toward God in intense and agonizing desire. Much of our modern prayer lacks power because it lacks heart. We rush into God's presence, run through a string of petitions, jump up, and go out. If someone asks us an hour later what we prayed for, often we cannot remember. If we put so little heart into our prayers, we cannot expect God to put much heart into answering them.

> PRAYER THAT PREVAILS WITH GOD IS PRAYER INTO WHICH WE PUT OUR WHOLE SOULS, STRETCHING OUT TOWARD GOD IN INTENSE AND AGONIZING DESIRE. MUCH OF OUR MODERN PRAYER LACKS POWER BECAUSE IT LACKS HEART.

We hear much in our day about the *rest* of faith, but there is not much said about the *fight* of faith in prayer. Those who want us to think that they have attained to some great height of faith and trust because they have never known any agony or conflict in prayer have surely gone beyond their Lord. They have even gone beyond the mightiest victors for God, both in effort and prayer, which the ages of Christian history have known. When we learn to come to God with an intensity of desire that wrings the soul, then we will know a power in prayer that most of us do not yet know.

PRAYER AND FASTING

How will we achieve this earnestness in prayer? Not by trying to work ourselves up into it. The true method is explained in Romans 8:26:

> *Likewise the Spirit also helpeth our infirmities: for we know not what we should pray for as we ought: but the Spirit itself maketh intercession for us with groanings which cannot be uttered.*

The earnestness that we work up in the energy of the flesh is a repulsive thing. The earnestness created in us by the Holy Spirit is pleasing to God. Here again, if we desire to pray correctly, we must look to the Spirit of God to teach us how to pray.

It is in this connection that fasting enters in. In Daniel 9:3, we read that Daniel set his face *"unto the Lord God, to seek by prayer and supplications, with fasting, and sackcloth, and ashes."* There are those who think that fasting belongs to the old dispensation. But when we look at Acts 14:23 and Acts 13:2–3, we find that it was practiced by earnest men of the apostolic day.

If we want to pray with power, we should pray with fasting. This, of course, does not mean that we should fast every time we pray. But there are times of emergency or special crisis, when sincere believers will withdraw even from the gratification of natural appetites that would be perfectly proper under other circumstances in order to give themselves up solely to prayer. There is a mysterious power in such prayer. Every great crisis in life and work should be met in that way. There is nothing pleasing to God in our giving up things that are pleasant in a purely Pharisaic or legalistic way. But there is power in that downright earnestness and determination to obtain, in prayer, the things that we strongly feel are needs. This feeling of urgency leads us to put away everything, even things that are normal and necessary, that we may set our faces to find God and obtain blessings from Him.

UNITY IN PRAYER

Another secret of proper praying is found in Acts 12:5. It appears in the three words *"of the church."* There is power in united prayer. Of course, there is power in the prayer of an individual, but there is much more power in united prayer. God delights in the unity of His people and seeks to emphasize it in every way. Thus, He pronounces a special blessing on corporate prayer. We read in Matthew 18:19, *"If two of you shall agree on earth as touching any thing that they shall ask, it shall be done for them of my Father which is in heaven."* This unity, however, must be real. The passage just quoted does not say that if two will agree in asking, but if two will agree as *"any thing that they shall ask."* Two people might agree to ask for the same thing, and yet there may be no real agreement concerning the thing they asked. One might ask it because he really desired it; the other might ask simply to please his friend. But where there is real agreement, where the Spirit of God brings believers into perfect harmony concerning what they ask of God, where the Spirit lays the same burden on two or more hearts, there is absolutely irresistible power in prayer.

CHAPTER 3

OBEYING AND PRAYING

One of the most significant verses in the Bible on prayer is 1 John 3:22. John said, *"And whatsoever we ask, we receive of him, because we keep his commandments, and do those things that are pleasing in his sight."* What an astounding statement! John said, in so many words, that he received everything he asked for. How many of us can say the same? But John explains why this was so: *"Because we keep his commandments, and do those things that are pleasing in his sight."* In other words, the one who expects God to do as he asks Him must do whatever God bids him. If we give a listening ear to all God's commands to us, He will give a listening ear to all our petitions to Him. If, on the other hand, we turn a deaf ear to His precepts, He will be likely to turn a deaf ear to our prayers. Here we find the secret of much unanswered prayer. We are not listening to God's Word; therefore, He is not listening to our petitions.

I was once speaking to a woman who had been a professed Christian but had given it all up. I asked her why she was not a Christian any longer. She replied, because she did not believe the Bible. I asked her why she did not believe the Bible.

"Because I have tried its promises and found them untrue."

"Which promises?"

"The promises about prayer."

"Which promises about prayer?"

"Does it not say in the Bible, *'Whatsoever ye shall ask in prayer, believing, ye shall receive'*" (Matthew 21:22)?

"It does say that."

"Well, I asked fully expecting to get and did not receive, so the promise failed."

"Was the promise made to you?"

"Why, certainly, it is made to all Christians, is it not?"

"No, God carefully defines who 'ye' is whose believing prayers He agrees to answer."

I then directed her to 1 John 3:22 and read the description of those whose prayers had power with God.

"Now," I said, "were you keeping His commandments and doing those things that are pleasing in His sight?"

She frankly confessed that she was not, and she soon came to see that the real difficulty was not with God's promises but with herself. That is the reason for many unanswered prayers today—the one who offers them is not obedient.

KNOWING AND DOING GOD'S WILL

If we want power in prayer, we must be earnest students of His Word to find out what His will regarding us is. Then having found it, we must do it. One unconfessed act of disobedience on our part will shut the ear of God against many petitions. But this verse goes beyond the mere keeping of God's commandments. John tells us that we must *do those things that are pleasing in his sight*" (1 John 3:22).

There are many things that would please God but which He has not specifically commanded. A true child is not content with merely doing those things that his father specifically commands him to do. He tries to know his father's will, and if he thinks that there is anything that he can do that would please his father, he does it gladly. He does so even if his father has never given him any specific order to do it. So it is with the true child of God. He does not merely ask whether certain things are commanded or certain things forbidden. He tries to know his Father's will in all things.

Many Christians today are doing things that are not pleasing to God. Many also neglect to do things that would be pleasing to God. When you speak to them about these things, they will confront you at once with the question "Is there any command in the Bible not to do this thing?" If you cannot show them the verse in which their action is plainly forbidden, they think they are under no obligation whatever to give it up. But a true child of God does not demand a specific command. If we make it our desire to find out and do the things that are pleasing to God, He will make it His desire to do the things that are pleasing to us. Here again we find the explanation of much unanswered prayer. We are not making it our desire to know what pleases our Father; thus, our prayers are not answered.

PRAYING IN TRUTH

Psalm 145:18 throws a great deal of light on the question of how to pray: *"The Lord is nigh unto all them that call upon him, to all that call upon him in truth."* That little expression *"in truth"* is worthy of further study. If you take your concordance and go through the Bible, you will find that this expression means "in reality," "in sincerity." The prayer that God answers is the prayer that is real, the prayer that asks for something that is sincerely desired.

Much of our prayer is insincere. People ask for things that they do not wish. Many women pray for the conversion of their husbands but do not really wish their husbands to be converted. They think they do, but if they knew what would be involved in the conversion of their husbands, they would think again. It would necessitate an entire revolution in their manner of doing business and would consequently reduce their income, making it necessary to change their entire way of living. If they were sincere with God, the real prayer of their hearts would be, "O God, do not convert my husband." Some women do not wish their husbands' conversion at so great a cost.

> REVIVAL BRINGS THE SEARCHING OF HEARTS ON THE PART OF PROFESSED CHRISTIANS, A RADICAL TRANSFORMATION OF INDIVIDUAL, HOME, AND SOCIAL LIFE, WHEN THE SPIRIT OF GOD IS POURED OUT IN REALITY AND POWER.

Many churches are praying for a revival but do not really desire a revival. They think they do, for in their minds, a revival means an increase of membership, income, and reputation among the churches. But if they knew what a real revival meant, they would not be so eager. Revival brings

the searching of hearts on the part of professed Christians, a radical transformation of individual, home, and social life, when the Spirit of God is
poured out in reality and power. If all this were known, the real cry of the
church would be, "O God, keep us from having a revival."

Many ministers are praying for the filling with the Holy Spirit, yet
they do not really desire it. They think they do, for the filling with the
Spirit means new joy and power in preaching the Word, a wider reputation among men, and a larger prominence in the church of Christ. But
if they understood what a filling with the Holy Spirit really involved,
they would think less about its rewards. They would think more of how
it would necessarily bring them into antagonism with the world, with
unspiritual Christians, how it would cause their name to be "cast out as
evil" (see Luke 6:22), and how it might necessitate their leaving a good,
comfortable living to go to work in the slums or even in some foreign land.
If they understood all this, their prayer most likely would be—if they
were to express the real wish of their hearts—"O God, save me from being
filled with the Holy Spirit."

When we do come to the place where we really desire the conversion of friends at any cost, really desire the outpouring of the Holy Spirit
whatever it may involve, really desire anything "*in truth,*" and then call
upon God for it "*in truth,*" God is going to hear.

CHAPTER 4

PRAYING IN THE NAME OF CHRIST

Jesus spoke a wonderful word about prayer to His disciples on the night before His crucifixion: *"Whatsoever ye shall ask in my name, that will I do, that the Father may be glorified in the Son. If ye shall ask any thing in my name, I will do it"* (John 14:13–14). Prayer in the name of Christ has power with God. God is well pleased with His Son Jesus Christ. He always hears Him, and He also always hears the prayer that is really in His name. There is a fragrance in the name of Christ that makes every prayer that bears it acceptable to God. But what is it to pray in the name of Christ?

Many explanations have been attempted that make little sense to the average person. But there is nothing mystical or mysterious about this expression. If you go through the Bible and examine all the passages in which the expressions "in My name" or "in His name" are used, you will find that they mean just about what they do in everyday language.

If I go to a bank and hand in a check with my name signed to it, I ask of that bank in my own name. If I have money deposited in that bank, the check will be cashed; if not, it will not be. If, however, I go to a bank with somebody else's name signed to the check, I am asking in his name, and it does not matter whether I have money in that bank or any other. If the person whose name is signed to the check has money there, the check will be cashed. For example, if I were to go to the First National Bank of Chicago and present a check that I had signed for five hundred dollars, the teller would say to me: "Why, Mr. Torrey, we cannot cash that. You have no money in this bank."

But if I were to go to the First National Bank with a check for five hundred dollars made payable to me and signed by one of the large depositors in that bank, they would not ask whether I had money in that bank or in any bank. Instead, they would honor the check at once.

When I go to God in prayer, it is like going to the bank of heaven. I have nothing deposited there. I have absolutely no credit there. If I go in my own name, I will get absolutely nothing. But Jesus Christ has unlimited credit in heaven, and He has granted me the privilege of going to the bank with His name on my checks. When I thus go, my prayers will be honored to any extent.

To pray in the name of Christ is to pray on the ground of His credit, not mine. It is to renounce the thought that I have any claims on God whatever and approach Him on the ground of Christ's claims. Praying in the name of Christ is not done by merely adding the phrase "I ask these things in Jesus' name" to my prayer. I may put that phrase in my prayer and really be resting in my own merit all the time. On the other hand, I may omit that phrase but really be resting in the merit of Christ all the time. When I really do approach God on the ground of Christ's merit and His atoning blood (see Hebrews 10:19), God will hear me. Many of our prayers are in vain because men approach God imagining that they have some claim that obligates Him to answer their prayers.

FORGIVENESS IN HIS NAME

Years ago, when D. L. Moody was young in Christian work, he visited a town in Illinois. A judge in the town was not a Christian. This judge's wife asked Mr. Moody to call on her husband, but he replied, "I cannot talk with your husband. I am only an uneducated, young Christian, and your husband is a scholarly nonbeliever."

But the wife would not take no for an answer, so Mr. Moody made the call. The clerks in the outer office giggled as the young salesman from Chicago went in to talk with the scholarly judge. The conversation was short. Mr. Moody said, "Judge, I can't talk with you. You are an educated non-Christian, and I have no learning. I simply want to say that if you are ever converted, I want you to let me know."

The judge replied, "Yes, young man, if I am ever converted, I will let you know."

The conversation ended. The clerks snickered louder when the zealous, young Christian left the office, but the judge was converted within a year. Mr. Moody, visiting the town again, asked the judge to explain how it came about. The judge said,

One night, when my wife was at prayer meeting, I began to grow very uneasy and miserable. I did not know what was the matter with me, but I finally retired before my wife came home. I could not sleep all that night. I got up early, told my wife that I would eat no breakfast, and went down to the office. I told the clerks they could take a holiday and shut myself up in the inner office. I kept growing more and more miserable, and finally I got down and asked God to forgive my sins. But I would not say, "For Jesus' sake" because I was a Unitarian and did not believe in the atonement. I kept praying, "God forgive my sins," but no answer came. At last, in desperation, I cried, "O God, for Christ's sake, forgive my sins" and found peace at once.

The judge had no access to God until he came in the name of Christ. When he finally came in the name of Jesus, he was heard and answered at once.

KNOWING GOD'S WILL THROUGH HIS WORD

Great light is thrown on how to pray by 1 John 5:14–15:

This is the confidence that we have in him, that, if we ask any thing according to his will, he heareth us: And if we know that he hear us, whatsoever we ask, we know that we have the petitions that we desired of him.

This passage clearly teaches that if we are to pray correctly, we must pray according to God's will. Then, we will, beyond a shadow of a doubt, receive the thing we ask of Him. But can we know the will of God? Can we know that any specific prayer is according to His will?

We most surely can. How? First by the Word. God has revealed His will in His Word. When anything is definitely promised in the Word of God, we know that it is His will to give that thing. If, when I pray, I can find some definite promise of God's Word and lay that promise before God, I know that He hears me. And if I know that He hears me, I know that I have the petition that I have asked of Him. For example, when I pray for wisdom, I know that it is the will of God to give me wisdom, for He said so in James 1:5: *"If any of you lack wisdom, let him ask of God, that giveth to all men liberally, and upbraideth not; and it shall be given him."* So when I ask for wisdom, I know that the prayer is heard and that wisdom will be given to me. In like manner, when I pray for the Holy Spirit, I know that it is God's will that my prayer is heard and that I have the petition that I have asked of Him: *"If ye then, being evil, know how to give good gifts unto your children: how much more shall your heavenly Father give the Holy Spirit to them that ask him?"* (Luke 11:13).

Some years ago, a minister came to me at the close of an address on prayer at a YMCA Bible school and said, "You have given those young men the impression that they can ask for definite things and get the very things that they ask."

I replied that I did not know whether that was the impression I had given or not, but that was certainly the impression I desired to give.

"But," he replied, "that is not right. We cannot be sure, for we don't know God's will."

I turned at once to James 1:5, read it to him, and said, "Is it not God's will to give us wisdom, and if you ask for wisdom, do you not know that you are going to get it?"

"Ah!" he said, "we don't know what wisdom is."

I said, "No, if we did, we would not need to ask. But whatever wisdom may be, don't you know that you will get it?"

Certainly it is our privilege to know. When we have a specific promise in the Word of God, if we doubt that it is God's will or if we doubt that God will do what we ask, we make God a liar. (See 1 John 5:10.)

Here is one of the greatest secrets of prevailing prayer: Study the Word to find what God's will is as revealed there in the promises. Then, simply take these promises and claim them before God in prayer with the absolutely unwavering expectation that He will do what He has promised in His Word.

KNOWING GOD'S WILL BY HIS SPIRIT

Another way in which we may know the will of God is by the teaching of His Holy Spirit. There are many things that we need from God that are not covered by any specific promise. But we are not in ignorance of the will of God even then. In Romans 8:26–27, we are told,

Likewise the Spirit also helpeth our infirmities: for we know not what we should pray for as we ought: but the Spirit itself maketh intercession for us with groanings which cannot be uttered. And he that searcheth the hearts knoweth what is the mind of the Spirit, because he maketh intercession for the saints according to the will of God.

> OFTEN, BY HIS SPIRIT, GOD LAYS A HEAVY BURDEN OF PRAYER FOR SOME GIVEN INDIVIDUAL ON OUR HEARTS. WE CANNOT REST.
> WE PRAY FOR HIM *"WITH GROANINGS WHICH CANNOT BE UTTERED."*
> PERHAPS THE MAN IS ENTIRELY BEYOND OUR REACH, BUT GOD HEARS THE PRAYER. AND, IN MANY CASES, IT IS NOT LONG BEFORE WE HEAR OF HIS DEFINITE CONVERSION.

Here we are distinctly told that the Spirit of God prays in us, draws out our prayers, according to God's will. When we are thus led out by the Holy Spirit in any direction, to pray for any given object, we may do it in all confidence that it is God's will. We are to be assured that we will receive the very thing we ask of Him, even though there is no specific promise to cover the case. Often, by His Spirit, God lays a heavy burden of prayer for some given individual on our hearts. We cannot rest. We pray for him *"with groanings which cannot be uttered."* Perhaps the man is entirely beyond our reach, but God hears the prayer. And, in many cases, it is not long before we hear of his definite conversion.

The passage in 1 John 5:14–15 is one of the most abused passages in the Bible:

This is the confidence that we have in him, that, if we ask any thing according to his will, he heareth us: and if we know that he hear us, whatsoever we ask, we know that we have the petitions that we desired of him.

Undoubtedly, the Holy Spirit put this passage into the Bible to encourage our faith. It begins with *"this is the confidence that we have in him,"* and closes with *"we know that we have the petitions that we desired of him."* But one of the most frequent usages of this passage, which was so clearly given to bring confidence, is to introduce an element of uncertainty into our prayers. Often, when a person is confident in prayer, some cautious brother will come and say, "Now, don't be too confident. If it is God's will, He will do it. You should add, 'If it be Your will.'"

Doubtless, there are many times when we do not know the will of God, and submission to the excellent will of God should be the basis for all prayer. But when we know God's will, there need be no ifs. This passage was not put into the Bible so that we could introduce *ifs* into all our prayers but so that we could throw our *ifs* to the wind and have *"confidence"* and *"know that we have the petitions that we desired of him."*

CHAPTER 5

PRAYING IN THE SPIRIT

Over and over again, we have seen our dependence on the Holy Spirit in prayer. This is stated very clearly in Ephesians 6:18: *"Praying always with all prayer and supplication in the Spirit"* and in Jude 20, *"Praying in the Holy Ghost."* Indeed, the whole secret of prayer is found in these three words: *"in the Spirit."* God the Father answers the prayers that God the Holy Spirit inspires.

The disciples did not know how to pray as they should, so they came to Jesus and said, *"Lord, teach us to pray"* (Luke 11:1). We also do not know how to pray as we should, but we have another Teacher and Guide right at hand to help us. (See John 14:16–17.) *"The Spirit also helpeth our infirmities"* (Romans 8:26). He teaches us how to pray. True prayer is prayer in the Spirit—that is, the prayer the Spirit inspires and directs. When we come into God's presence, we should recognize our infirmities, our ignorance of what we should pray for, or how we should pray for it. In the consciousness of our utter inability to pray properly, we should look to the Holy Spirit, casting ourselves completely on Him to direct our prayers. He must lead our desires and guide our expressions of them.

Nothing can be more foolish in prayer than to rush heedlessly into God's presence and ask the first thing that comes into our minds. When we first come into God's presence, we should be silent before Him. We should look to Him to send His Holy Spirit to teach us how to pray. We must wait for the Holy Spirit and surrender ourselves to the Spirit. Then, we will pray correctly.

Often, when we come to God in prayer, we do not feel like praying. What should we do in such a case? Stop praying until we feel like it? Not at all. When we feel least like praying is the time when we most need to pray. We should wait quietly before God and tell Him how cold and prayerless our hearts are. We should look to Him, trust Him, and expect

Him to send the Holy Spirit to warm our hearts and draw us out in prayer. It will not be long before the glow of the Spirit's presence will fill our hearts. We will begin to pray with freedom, directness, earnestness, and power. Many of the most blessed seasons of prayer I have ever known have begun with a feeling of utter deadness and prayerlessness. But in my helplessness and coldness, I have cast myself on God and looked to Him to send His Holy Spirit to teach me to pray. And He has always done it.

When we pray in the Spirit, we will pray for the right things in the right way. There will be joy and power in our prayers.

PRAYING WITH FAITH

If we are to pray with power, we must pray with faith. In Mark 11:24, Jesus said, *"Therefore I say unto you, What things soever ye desire, when ye pray, believe that ye receive them, and ye shall have them."* No matter how positive any promise of God's Word may be, we will not enjoy it unless we confidently expect its fulfillment. James said, *"If any of you lack wisdom, let him ask of God, that giveth to all men liberally, and upbraideth not; and it shall be given him"* (James 1:5). Now, that promise is as positive as a promise can be. The next two verses add:

> But let him ask in faith, nothing wavering. For he that wavereth is like a wave of the sea driven with the wind and tossed. For let not that man think that he shall receive any thing of the Lord.
> (James 1:6–7)

There must then be confident, unwavering expectation.

But there is a faith that goes beyond expectation. It believes that prayer is heard and that the promise is granted. This comes out in Mark 11:24: *"Therefore I say unto you, What things soever ye desire, when ye pray, believe that ye receive them, and ye shall have them."* But how can one have this kind of faith?

Let us say with all emphasis, it cannot be forced. A person reads this promise about the prayer of faith and then asks for things that he desires. He tries to make himself believe that God has heard the prayer. This only ends in disappointment. It is not real faith, and the thing is not granted. At this point, many people lose faith altogether by trying to create faith by an effort of their will. When the thing they made themselves believe they would receive is not given, the very foundation of faith is often undermined.

But how does real faith come? Romans 10:17 answers the question: *"So then faith cometh by hearing, and hearing by the word of God."* If we are to have real faith, we must study the Word of God and discover what is promised. Then, we must simply believe the promises of God. Faith must have God's sanction. Trying to believe something that you want to believe is not faith. Believing what God says in His Word is faith. If I am to have faith when I pray, I must find some promise in the Word of God to rest my faith on.

> FAITH MUST HAVE GOD'S SANCTION. TRYING TO BELIEVE SOMETHING THAT YOU WANT TO BELIEVE IS NOT FAITH. BELIEVING WHAT GOD SAYS IN HIS WORD IS FAITH.

Furthermore, faith comes through the Spirit. The Spirit knows the will of God. If I pray in the Spirit and look to the Spirit to teach me God's will, He will lead me in prayer according to the will of God. He will give me faith that the prayer is to be answered. But in no case does real faith come by simply determining that you are going to receive what you want. If there is no promise in the Word of God and no clear leading of the Spirit, there can be no real faith. There should be no scolding for your lack of faith in such a case. But if the thing desired is promised in the Word of God, we may well scold ourselves for lack of faith if we doubt, for we are making God a liar by doubting His Word.

CHAPTER 6

ALWAYS PRAYING AND NOT FAINTING

In the gospel of Luke, Jesus emphasized the lesson that men should always pray and not faint. (See Luke 18:1). The first parable is found in Luke 11:5–8 and the other in Luke 18:1–8.

> *He said unto them, Which of you shall have a friend, and shall go unto him at midnight, and say unto him, Friend, lend me three loaves; for a friend of mine in his journey is come to me, and I have nothing to set before him? And he from within shall answer and say, Trouble me not: the door is now shut, and my children are with me in bed; I cannot rise and give thee. I say unto you, Though he will not rise and give him, because he is his friend, yet because of his importunity he will rise and give him as many as he needeth.* (Luke 11:5–8)

> *He spake a parable unto them to this end, that men ought always to pray, and not to faint; saying, There was in a city a judge, which feared not God, neither regarded man: and there was a widow in that city; and she came unto him, saying, Avenge me of mine adversary. And he would not for a while: but afterward he said within himself, Though I fear not God, nor regard man; yet because this widow troubleth me, I will avenge her, lest by her continual coming she weary me. And the Lord said, Hear what the unjust judge saith. And shall not God avenge his own elect, which cry day and night unto him, though he bear long with them? I tell you that he will avenge them speedily. Nevertheless when the Son of man cometh, shall he find faith on the earth?* (Luke 18:1–8)

In the former of these two parables, Jesus sets forth in a startling way the necessity of persistence in prayer. The word translated *"importunity"* literally means "shamelessness." Jesus wants us to understand that God desires us to draw near to Him with a determination to obtain the things we seek that will not be put to shame by any seeming refusal or delay on God's part. God delights in the holy boldness that will not take no for an answer. It is an expression of great faith, and nothing pleases God more than faith.

> GOD DELIGHTS IN THE HOLY BOLDNESS THAT WILL NOT TAKE NO FOR AN ANSWER. IT IS AN EXPRESSION OF GREAT FAITH, AND NOTHING PLEASES GOD MORE THAN FAITH.

Jesus seemed to deal with the Syro-Phoenician woman almost with rudeness. But she would not give up that easily, and Jesus looked on her shameless persistence with pleasure. He said, *"O woman, great is thy faith: be it unto thee even as thou wilt"* (Matthew 15:28). God does not always give us things at our first efforts. He wants to train us and make us strong by compelling us to work hard for the best things. Likewise, He does not always give us what we ask in answer to the first prayer. He wants to train us and make us strong people of prayer by compelling us to pray hard for the best things. He makes us pray through.

I am glad that this is so. There is no more blessed training in prayer than what comes through being compelled to ask again and again, over long periods of time, before obtaining what we seek from God. Many people call it submission to the will of God when God does not grant them their requests at the first or second asking. They say, "Well, perhaps it is not God's will."

As a rule, this is not submission but spiritual laziness. We do not call it submission to the will of God when we give up after one or two efforts to obtain things by action. We call it lack of strength of character. When the strong man or woman of action starts out to accomplish a thing and does not accomplish it the first or second or one-hundredth time, he or she keeps hammering away until it is accomplished. The strong person of prayer keeps on praying until he prays through and obtains what he seeks. We should be careful about what we ask from God. But when we do begin to pray for a thing, we should never give up praying for it until we receive it or until God makes it very clear and very definite that it is not His will to give it.

Some people like us to believe that it shows unbelief to pray twice for the same thing. They think we ought to claim the answer the first time we ask. Doubtless, there are times when we are able, through faith in the Word or the leading of the Holy Spirit, to claim the first time what we have asked of God. But beyond question, there are other times when we must pray again and again for the same thing before we receive our answers. Those who are beyond praying twice for the same thing are beyond following their Master's example. (See Matthew 26:44.)

George Müller prayed for two men daily for more than sixty years. Although both were eventually converted, one turned to the Lord shortly before George Müller's death, I think at the last service that George Müller held. The other was converted within a year after Müller's death. One of the great needs of the present day is for men and women who will not only start out to pray for things but will pray on and on until they obtain what they seek from the Lord.

CHAPTER 7

ABIDING IN CHRIST

The whole secret of prayer is found in these words of our Lord: *"If ye abide in me, and my words abide in you, ye shall ask what ye will, and it shall be done unto you"* (John 15:7). Here is prayer that has unbounded power: *"Ask what ye will, and it shall be done unto you."*

There is a way, then, of asking and receiving precisely what we ask. Christ gives two conditions for this all-prevailing prayer. The first condition is *"If ye abide in me."* What does it mean to abide in Christ? Some explanations are so mystical or so profound that many children of God think they mean practically nothing at all. But what Jesus meant was really very simple.

He had been comparing Himself to a vine and His disciples to the branches in the vine. Some branches continued in the vine in living union so that the sap or life of the vine constantly flowed into the branches. They had no independent life of their own. Everything in them was simply the outcome of the life of the vine flowing into them. Their buds, leaves, blossoms, and fruit were not really theirs but the buds, leaves, blossoms, and fruit of the vine. Other branches were completely severed from the vine, or the flow of the sap or life of the vine was in some way hindered.

For us to abide in Christ is to bear the same relationship to Him that the first sort of branches bear to the vine. That is to say, to abide in Christ is to renounce any independent lives of our own. We must give up trying to think our own thoughts, form our own resolutions, or cultivate our own feelings. We must simply and constantly look to Christ to think His thoughts in us, to form His purposes in us, to feel His emotions and affections in us. It is to renounce all life independent of Christ and constantly look to Him for the inflow of His life into us and the outworking of His life through us. When we do this, our prayers will obtain what we seek from God.

This must necessarily be so, for our desires will not be our own desires but Christ's. And our prayers will not in reality be our own prayers but Christ praying in us. Such prayers will always be in harmony with God's will, and the Father always hears Him. When our prayers fail, it is because they are indeed our prayers. We have conceived the desire and offered our own petitions instead of looking to Christ to pray through us.

To abide in Christ, one must already be in Christ through the acceptance of Christ as an atoning Savior from the guilt of sin. Christ must be acknowledged as a risen Savior from the power of sin and as Lord and Master over all the believer's life. Once we are in Christ, all that we have to do to abide in Christ is simply to renounce our self-life. We must utterly renounce every thought, purpose, desire, and affection of our own and continually look for Jesus Christ to form His thoughts, purposes, affections, and desires in us. Abiding in Christ is really a very simple matter, though it is a wonderful life of privilege and of power.

CHRIST'S WORDS IN US

Another condition is stated in John 15:7, though it is really involved in the first: *"and my words abide in you."* If we are to receive from God all we ask from Him, Christ's words must abide in us. We must study His words and let them sink into our thoughts and hearts. We must keep them in our memories, obey them constantly in our lives, and let them shape and mold our daily lives and all our actions.

This is really the method of abiding in Christ. It is through His words that Jesus imparts Himself to us. The words He speaks to us are spirit and life. (See John 6:63.) It is vain to expect power in prayer unless we meditate on the words of Christ and let them sink deeply and find a permanent abode in our hearts. Many wonder why they are so powerless in prayer. The very simple explanation of it all is found in their neglect of the words of Christ. They have not hidden His words in their hearts (see Psalm 119:11); His words do not abide in them. It is not by moments of mystical meditation and rapturous experiences that we learn to abide in Christ. It is by feeding on His Word, His written word in the Bible, and looking to the Spirit to implant these words in our hearts to make them a living thing in our hearts. If we thus let the words of Christ abide in us, they will stir us up to prayer. They will be the mold in which our prayers are shaped. And our prayers will necessarily be consistent with God's will and will prevail with Him. Prevailing prayer is almost an impossibility where there is neglect of the study of God's Word.

> IF WE THUS LET THE WORDS OF CHRIST ABIDE IN US, THEY WILL STIR US UP TO PRAYER. THEY WILL BE THE MOLD IN WHICH OUR PRAYERS ARE SHAPED. AND OUR PRAYERS WILL NECESSARILY BE CONSISTENT WITH GOD'S WILL AND WILL PREVAIL WITH HIM.

Mere intellectual study of the Word of God is not enough; there must be meditation on it. The Word of God must be revolved over and over in the mind with a constant looking to God and His Spirit to make that Word a living thing in the heart. The prayer that is born of meditation on the Word of God is the prayer that soars upward to God's listening ear.

George Müller, one of the mightiest men of prayer, would begin praying by reading and meditating on God's Word until a prayer began to form itself in his heart. Thus, God Himself was the real author of the prayer, and God answered the prayer that He Himself had inspired.

The Word of God is the instrument through which the Holy Spirit works. It is the *"sword of the Spirit"* (Ephesians 6:17) in more senses than one. The person who wants to know the work of the Holy Spirit in any direction must feed on the Word. The person who desires to pray in the Spirit must meditate on the Word so that the Holy Spirit may have something through which He can work. The Holy Spirit works His prayers in us through the Word. Neglect of the Word makes praying in the Holy Spirit an impossibility. If we seek to feed the fire of our prayers with the fuel of God's Word, all our difficulties in prayer will disappear.

CHAPTER 8

PRAYING WITH THANKSGIVING

Two words are often overlooked in the lesson about prayer that Paul gives us in Philippians 4:6–7:

> *Be careful for nothing; but in every thing by prayer and supplication with thanksgiving let your requests be made known unto God. And the peace of God, which passeth all understanding, shall keep your hearts and minds through Christ Jesus.*

The two important words often disregarded are *"with thanksgiving."*

In approaching God to ask for new blessings, we must never forget to thank Him for blessings already granted. If we would just stop and think about how many prayers God has answered and how seldom we have thanked Him, I am sure we would be overwhelmed. We should be just as definite in returning thanks as we are in making our requests. We come to God with very specific petitions, but when we thank Him, our thanksgiving is indefinite and general.

Doubtless one reason why so many of our prayers lack power is because we have neglected to thank God for blessings already received. If anyone were to constantly ask us for help and never say "Thank you" for the help given, we would soon get tired of helping one so ungrateful. Indeed, our respect for the one we were helping would stop us from encouraging such rank ingratitude. Doubtless our heavenly Father, out of wise regard for our highest welfare, often refuses to answer our prayers in order to bring us to a sense of our ingratitude. We must be taught to be thankful.

God is deeply grieved by the thanklessness and ingratitude of which so many of us are guilty. When Jesus healed the ten lepers and only one came back to give Him thanks, in wonderment and pain, He exclaimed,

"Were there not ten cleansed? But where are the nine?" (Luke 17:17). How often He looks down on us in sadness at our forgetfulness of His repeated blessings and frequent answers to prayer.

> AS ONE MEDITATES ON THE ANSWERS TO PRAYERS ALREADY GRANTED, FAITH GROWS BOLDER AND BOLDER. IN THE VERY DEPTHS OF OUR SOULS, WE COME TO FEEL THAT NOTHING IS TOO HARD FOR THE LORD.

Returning thanks for blessings already received increases our faith and enables us to approach God with new boldness and new assurance. Doubtless the reason so many have so little faith when they pray is because they take so little time to meditate on and thank God for blessings already received. As one meditates on the answers to prayers already granted, faith grows bolder and bolder. In the very depths of our souls, we come to feel that nothing is too hard for the Lord. As we reflect on the wondrous goodness of God on the one hand and on the little thanksgiving offered on the other hand, we may well humble ourselves before God and confess our sins.

The mighty men of prayer in the Bible, and those throughout the ages of the church's history, have been men who were devoted to offering thanksgiving and praise. David was a mighty man of prayer, and his psalms abound with thanksgiving and praise. The apostles were mighty men of prayer. We read that they *"were continually in the temple, praising and blessing God"* (Luke 24:53). Paul was a mighty man of prayer. Often in his epistles, he burst out in specific thanksgiving to God for definite blessings and definite answers to prayers.

Jesus is our model in prayer as in everything else. In the study of His life, His manner of returning thanks at the simplest meal was so noticeable that two of His disciples recognized Him by this act after His resurrection. Thanksgiving is one of the inevitable results of being filled with the Holy Spirit. One who does not learn to *"in every thing give thanks"* (1 Thessalonians 5:18) cannot continue to pray in the Spirit. If we want to learn to pray with power, we would do well to let these two words sink deeply into our hearts: *"with thanksgiving."*

CHAPTER 9

HINDRANCES TO PRAYER

We have very carefully studied the positive conditions of prevailing prayer, but there are some things that hinder prayer. God has made these obstacles very plain in His Word.

SELFISH PRAYERS

The first hindrance to prayer is found in James 4:3: "*Ye ask, and receive not, because ye ask amiss, that ye may consume it upon your lusts.*" A selfish purpose in prayer robs prayer of power. Many prayers are selfish. These may be prayers for things for which it is perfectly proper to ask, for things which it is the will of God to give, but the motive of the prayer is entirely wrong, so the prayer falls powerless to the ground. The true purpose in prayer is that God may be glorified in the answer. If we ask any petition merely to receive something to use for our pleasure or gratification, we "*ask amiss*" and should not expect to receive what we ask. This explains why many prayers remain unanswered.

For example, a woman is praying for the conversion of her husband. That certainly is a most proper thing to ask. But her motive in asking for the conversion of her husband is entirely improper; it is selfish. She desires that her husband may be converted because it would be so much more pleasant for her to have a husband who sympathized with her. Or it is so painful to think that her husband might die and be lost forever. For some such selfish reason as this, she desires to have her husband converted. The prayer is purely selfish. Why should a woman desire the conversion of her husband? First and above all, that God may be glorified. It should be her desire because she cannot bear the thought that God the Father would be dishonored by her husband.

Many pray for a revival. That certainly is a prayer that is pleasing to God and in line with His will. But many prayers for revivals are purely selfish. Some churches desire revivals so that their membership may be increased or so that their church may have more power and influence in the community. Some churches want revival so that the church treasury may be filled or so that a good report may be made at the presbytery, conference, or association. For such low purposes as these, churches and ministers are often praying for a revival, and God does not answer the prayer.

We should pray for a revival because we cannot endure the dishonor of God caused by the worldliness of the church, the sins of unbelievers, and the proud unbelief of the day. We should pray for revival because God's Word is being made void. We should pray for revival so that God may be glorified by the outpouring of His Spirit on the church of Christ. For these reasons, first and above all, we should pray for revival.

Many prayers for filling by the Holy Spirit are selfish requests. It certainly is God's will to give the Holy Spirit to those who ask Him. He has told us so plainly in His Word. (See Luke 11:13.) But many prayers for filling by the Holy Spirit are hindered by the selfishness of the motive behind the prayer. Men and women pray for the Holy Spirit so that they may be happy, saved from the wretchedness of their lives, have power as Christian workers, or for some other self-centered reason. We should pray for the Holy Spirit in order that God may no longer be dishonored by the low level of our Christian lives and by our ineffective service. We should pray for the Holy Spirit so that God may be glorified in the new beauty that comes into our lives and the new power that comes into our service.

SIN HINDERS PRAYER

The second hindrance to prayer is seen in Isaiah 59:1–2:

Behold, the LORD's hand is not shortened, that it cannot save; neither his ear heavy, that it cannot hear: but your iniquities have separated between you and your God, and your sins have hid his face from you, that he will not hear.

Sin hinders prayer. Perhaps a man prays and prays and receives no answer to his prayers. Perhaps he is tempted to think that it is not the will of God to answer, or he may think that the days when God answered prayer are over. This is what the Israelites seem to have thought. They thought that the Lord's hand was shortened, that it could not save, and that His ear could no longer hear.

"Not so," said Isaiah. "God's ear is just as open to hear as ever; His hand is just as mighty to save. But there is a hindrance. That hindrance is your own sins. Your iniquities have separated you and your God. Your sins have hid His face from you so that He will not hear."

It is the same today. A man is crying to God in vain, simply because of sin in his life. It may be some sin in the past that has been unconfessed and unjudged. It may be some sin in the present that is cherished. Very likely, it is not even looked on as sin. But the sin is there, hidden away somewhere in the heart or in the life, and God *"will not hear."* Anyone who finds his prayers unanswered should not think that what he asks of God is not according to His will. Instead, he should go alone to God with the psalmist's prayer, *"Search me, O God, and know my heart: try me, and know my thoughts: and see if there be any wicked way in me"* (Psalm 139:23–24). He should wait before Him until He puts His finger on the thing that is displeasing in His sight. Then, this sin should be confessed and renounced.

I well remember a time in my life when I was praying for two definite things that I thought I must have, or God would be dishonored. But the answer did not come. I awoke in the middle of the night in great physical suffering and distress of soul. I cried to God for these things, reasoned with Him as to how necessary it was that I get them, and get them at once. Still no answer came. I asked God to show me if there was anything wrong in my own life. Something came to my mind that had often come to it before—something definite, which I was unwilling to confess as sin. I said to God, "If this is wrong, I will give it up." Still no answer came. Though I had never admitted it, in my innermost heart, I knew it was wrong.

> SIN IS AN AWFUL THING. ONE OF THE MOST AWFUL THINGS ABOUT IT IS THE WAY IT HINDERS PRAYER. IT SEVERS THE CONNECTION BETWEEN US AND THE SOURCE OF ALL GRACE, POWER, AND BLESSING. ANYONE WHO DESIRES POWER IN PRAYER MUST BE MERCILESS IN DEALING WITH HIS OWN SINS.

At last I said, "This is wrong. I have sinned. I will give it up." I found peace, and in a few moments, I was sleeping like a child. In the morning, the money that was needed so much for the honor of God's name came.

Sin is an awful thing. One of the most awful things about it is the way it hinders prayer. It severs the connection between us and the source of all grace, power, and blessing. Anyone who desires power in prayer must be merciless in dealing with his own sins. *"If I regard iniquity in my heart, the Lord will not hear"* (Psalm 66:18). As long as we hold on to sin or have any controversy with God, we cannot expect Him to heed our prayers. If there is anything that is constantly coming up in your moments of close communion with God, that is the thing that hinders prayer. Put it away.

WHO COMES FIRST?

The third hindrance to prayer is found in Ezekiel 14:3: *"Son of man, these men have set up their idols in their heart, and put the stumblingblock of their iniquity before their face: should I be enquired of at all by them?"* Idols in the heart cause God to refuse to listen to our prayers.

What is an idol? An idol is anything that takes the place of God, anything that is the ultimate object of our affections. God alone has the right to the supreme place in our hearts. Everything and everyone else must be subordinate to Him.

Suppose a man makes an idol of his wife. Not that a man can love his wife too much, but he can put her in the wrong place. He can put her before God. When a man regards his wife's pleasure before God's pleasure, when he gives her first place and God second place, his wife is an idol. God cannot hear his prayers.

Suppose a woman makes an idol of her children. Not that we can love our children too much. The more dearly we love Christ, the more dearly we love our children. But we can put our children in the wrong place; we can put them before God and their interests before God's interests. When we do this, our children become our idols.

Many make an idol of their reputations or careers. If these things come before God, God cannot hear the prayers of such people.

If we really desire power in prayer, we must answer the question "Is God absolutely first?" Is He before our wives, before our children, before our reputations, before our careers, before our own lives? If not, prevailing prayer is impossible.

God often calls our attention to the fact that we have an idol by not answering our prayers. Thus, He leads us to inquire as to why our prayers are not answered. And so, we discover the idol, renounce it, and then God hears our prayers.

GIVE IN ORDER TO RECEIVE

The fourth hindrance to prayer is found in Proverbs 21:13: *"Whoso stoppeth his ears at the cry of the poor, he also shall cry himself, but shall not be heard."* There is perhaps no greater hindrance to prayer than stinginess, the lack of generosity toward the poor and toward God's work. It is the one who gives generously to others who receives generously from God:

> Give, and it shall be given unto you; good measure, pressed down, and shaken together, and running over, shall men give into your bosom. For with the same measure that ye mete withal it shall be measured to you again.   (Luke 6:38)

The generous man is the mighty man of prayer. The stingy man is the powerless man of prayer.

One of the most wonderful statements about prevailing prayer is made in direct connection with generosity toward the needy: *"Whatsoever we ask, we receive of him, because we keep his commandments, and do those things that are pleasing in his sight"* (1 John 3:22). We are told in the context of the verse that when we love, not *"in word, neither in tongue; but in deed and in truth"* (verse 18), when we open our hearts toward the *"brother* [in] *need"* (verse 17), God hears us. It is only then that we have confidence toward God in prayer.

Many men and women are seeking to find the secret of their powerlessness in prayer. They need not seek far. It is nothing more nor less than downright stinginess. George Müller was a mighty man of prayer because he was a mighty giver. What he received from God never stuck to his fingers. He immediately passed it on to others. He was constantly receiving because he was constantly giving. When one thinks of the selfishness of the professing church today, it is no wonder that the church has so little power in prayer. If we want to receive from God, we must give to others. Perhaps the most wonderful promise in the Bible in regard to God's supplying our needs is Philippians 4:19: *"My God shall supply all your need according to his riches in glory by Christ Jesus.*" This glorious promise was made to the Philippian church and made in immediate connection with their generosity.

AN UNFORGIVING SPIRIT

The fifth hindrance to prayer is found in Mark 11:25: "*When ye stand praying, forgive, if ye have ought against any: that your Father also which is in heaven may forgive you your trespasses.*"

> GOD CANNOT DEAL WITH US ON THE BASIS OF FORGIVENESS WHILE WE ARE HARBORING ILL WILL AGAINST THOSE WHO HAVE WRONGED US. ANYONE WHO IS NURSING A GRUDGE AGAINST ANOTHER HAS CLOSED THE EAR OF GOD AGAINST HIS OWN PETITION.

An unforgiving spirit is one of the most common hindrances to prayer. Prayer is answered on the basis that our sins are forgiven. However, God cannot deal with us on the basis of forgiveness while we are harboring ill will against those who have wronged us. Anyone who is nursing a grudge against another has closed the ear of God against his own petition. How many are crying to God for the conversion of their husband, children, or friends and are wondering why it is that their prayers are not answered? The whole secret to their dilemma is some grudge that they have in their hearts against someone who has injured them. Many mothers and fathers allow their children to go through to eternity unsaved for the miserable gratification of hating somebody.

HUSBAND AND WIFE RELATIONSHIP

The sixth hindrance to prayer is found in 1 Peter 3:7:

> *Likewise, ye husbands, dwell with* [your wives] *according to knowledge, giving honour unto the wife, as unto the weaker vessel, and as being heirs together of the grace of life; that your prayers be not hindered.*

Here we are plainly told that a wrong relationship between husband and wife is a hindrance to prayer.

In many cases, the prayers of husbands are hindered because of their failure in duty toward their wives. On the other hand, without a doubt, it is true that the prayers of wives are hindered because of their failure in duty toward their husbands. If husbands and wives diligently seek to find the cause of their unanswered prayers, they will often find it in their relationship to one another.

Many men make great claims of holiness and are very active in Christian work but show little consideration in the treatment of their wives. It is often unkind, if not brutal. Then they wonder why their prayers are not answered. The verse that we have just read explains the seeming mystery. On the other hand, many women are very devoted to the church and very faithful in attendance, yet they treat their husbands with the most unpardonable neglect. They are cross and peevish toward them and wound them by the sharpness of their speech and unruly temper. Then they wonder why they have no power in prayer.

Other things in the relationship between husbands and wives cannot be spoken of publicly but are often hindrances in approaching God in prayer. There is much sin covered up under the holy name of marriage. This sin is a cause of spiritual deadness and of powerlessness in prayer. Men or women whose prayers seem to bring no answer should spread their whole married life out before God. They should ask Him to put His finger on anything that is displeasing in His sight.

BELIEVE HIS WORD ABSOLUTELY

The seventh hindrance to prayer is found in James 1:5–7:

> If any of you lack wisdom, let him ask of God, that giveth to all men liberally, and upbraideth not; and it shall be given him. But let him ask in faith, nothing wavering. For he that wavereth is like a wave of the sea driven with the wind and tossed. For let not that man think that he shall receive any thing of the Lord.

Prayers are hindered by unbelief. God demands that we believe His Word absolutely. To question it is to make Him a liar. (See 1 John 5:10.) Many of us do that when we plead His promises. Is it any wonder that our prayers are not answered? How many prayers are hindered by our wretched unbelief? We go to God and ask Him for something that is positively promised in His Word, and then we only half expect to get it. "Let not that man think that he shall receive any thing of the Lord."

CHAPTER 10

WHEN TO PRAY

If we want to know the fullness of blessing in our prayer lives, it is important not only to pray in the right way but also at the right time. Christ's own example is full of suggestions as to the right time for prayer. In the first chapter of Mark, we read: *"In the morning, rising up a great while before day, he went out, and departed into a solitary place, and there prayed"* (verse 35).

PRAYER IN THE MORNING

Jesus chose the early morning hour for prayer. Many of the mightiest men of God have followed the Lord's example in this. In the morning hour, the mind is fresh and at its very best. It is free from distraction. That absolute concentration that is essential to the most effective prayer is most easily possible in the early morning hours. Furthermore, when the early hours are spent in prayer, the whole day is sanctified. Power is then obtained for overcoming life's temptations and for performing its duties. More can be accomplished in prayer in the first hours of the day than at any other time. Every child of God who wants to make the most out of his life for Christ should set apart the first part of the day to meet with God in the study of His Word and in prayer. The first thing we do each day should be to get alone with God. We can then face the duties, the temptations, and the service of that day and receive strength from God for all. We should get victory before the hour of trial, temptation, or service comes. The secret place of prayer is the place to fight our battles and gain our victories.

NIGHTS OF PRAYER

In Luke, we find further light regarding the right time to pray: *"It came to pass in those days, that he went out into a mountain to pray, and continued all night in prayer to God"* (Luke 6:12). Here we see Jesus praying at night, spending the entire night in prayer. Of course, we have no reason to suppose that this was the constant practice of our Lord, nor do we even know how common this practice was. But there were certainly times when the whole night was given up to prayer. Here, too, we would do well to follow in the footsteps of the Master.

Of course, there is a way of setting apart nights for prayer in which there is no profit. It is pure legalism. But the abuse of this practice is no reason for neglecting it altogether. One should not say, "I am going to spend a whole night in prayer," thinking that there is any merit that will win God's favor in such an exercise. That is legalism. But we often do well to say, "I am going to set apart this night for meeting God and obtaining His blessing and power. If necessary, and if He so leads me, I will give the whole night to prayer." Often, we will have prayed things through long before the night has passed. Then we can retire and enjoy more refreshing and invigorating sleep than if we had not spent the time in prayer. At other times, God will keep us in communion with Himself way into the morning. When He does this in His infinite grace, these hours of night prayer are blessed indeed.

Nights of prayer to God are followed by days of power with men. In the night hours, the world is hushed in slumber. We can easily be alone with God and have undisturbed communion with Him. If we set apart the whole night for prayer, there will be no hurry. There will be time for our own hearts to become quiet before God. There will be time for the whole mind to be brought under the guidance of the Holy Spirit. There will be plenty of time to pray things through. A night of prayer should be put entirely under God's control. We should lay down no rules as to how long we will pray or what we will pray about. Be ready to wait on God for as short or as long a time as He may lead. Be ready to be led in one direction or another as He sees fit.

PRAYER BEFORE AND AFTER A CRISIS

Jesus Christ prayed before all the great crises in earthly life. He prayed before His entrance into His public ministry. (See Luke 3:21–22.) He prayed before choosing the twelve disciples. (See Luke 6:12–13.) He prayed during His public ministry. (See, for example, Mark 1:35–38.) He prayed before announcing to the Twelve His approaching death (see Luke 9:18, 21–22) and before the great consummation of His life on the cross (see Luke 22:39–46). He prepared for every important crisis by a lengthy season of prayer. We should do likewise. When any crisis of life is seen to be approaching, we should prepare for it by a season of very definite prayer to God. We should take plenty of time for this prayer.

Christ prayed not only before the great events and victories of His life but also after its great achievements and important crises. When He had fed the five thousand with the five loaves and two fishes, the multitude desired to take Him and make Him king. Having sent them away, He went up into the mountain to pray and spent hours there alone with God. (See Matthew 14:23; John 6:15.) So He went on from victory to victory.

> WHEN ANY CRISIS OF LIFE IS SEEN TO BE APPROACHING, WE SHOULD PREPARE FOR IT BY A SEASON OF VERY DEFINITE PRAYER TO GOD. WE SHOULD TAKE PLENTY OF TIME FOR THIS PRAYER.

It is more common for most of us to pray before the great events of life than it is to pray after them. But the latter is as important as the former. If we prayed after the great achievements of life, we might go on to still greater accomplishments. As it is, we are often either exalted or exhausted by the things that we do in the name of the Lord, and so we advance no further. Often, a man, in answer to prayer, has been endued with power and has thus worked great things in the name of the Lord. When these great things were accomplished, instead of going alone with God and humbling himself before Him, giving God the glory, he has congratulated himself. He has become arrogant, and God has been obliged to lay him aside. The great things done were not followed by humility and thanks to God. Thus, pride entered, and the man was stripped of his power.

NEVER TOO BUSY

Jesus Christ gave special time to prayer when He was unusually busy. He would withdraw from the multitudes that thronged about Him and go into the wilderness to pray. For example, we read in Luke 5:15–16:

But so much the more went there a fame abroad of him: and great multitudes came together to hear, and to be healed by him of their infirmities. And he withdrew himself into the wilderness, and prayed..

Some men are so busy that they find no time for prayer. Apparently, the busier Christ's life was, the more He prayed. Sometimes He had no time to eat. (See Mark 3:20.) Sometimes He had no time for needed rest and sleep. (See Mark 6:31, 33, 46.) But He always took time to pray. The more the work increased, the more He prayed.

Many mighty followers of God have learned this secret from Christ. And when the work has increased more than usual, they have set an unusual amount of time apart for prayer. Other people of God, once mighty, have lost their power because they did not learn this secret. They allowed increasing work to crowd out prayer.

Years ago, it was my privilege, with other theological students, to ask questions of one of the most helpful Christian men of the day. I was led to ask, "Will you tell us something of your prayer life?"

The man was silent a moment, and then, turning his eyes earnestly upon me, replied, "Well, I must admit that I have been so swamped with work lately that I have not given the time I should to prayer."

Is it any wonder that man lost power? The great work he was doing was curtailed in a very marked degree. Let us never forget that the more work pressures us, the more time we must spend in prayer.

PRAY AT ALL TIMES

Jesus Christ prayed before the great temptations of His life.

As He drew nearer and nearer to the cross and realized that the great final test of His life was imminent, Jesus went out into the garden to pray. He came *"unto a place called Gethsemane, and saith unto the disciples, Sit ye here, while I go and pray yonder"* (Matthew 26:36). The victory of Calvary was won that night in the garden of Gethsemane. The calm majesty with which He bore the awful onslaughts of Pilate's judgment hall and Calvary resulted from the struggle, agony, and victory of Gethsemane. While Jesus prayed, the disciples slept. He stood fast while they fell dishonorably.

Many temptations come on us suddenly and unannounced. All we can do is lift a cry to God for help then and there. But many temptations of life we can see ahead of time, and in such cases, the victory should be won before the temptation really reaches us.

In 1 Thessalonians 5:17, we read, *"Pray without ceasing,"* and in Ephesians 6:18, *"Praying always."* Our whole lives should be lives of prayer. We should walk in constant communion with God. There should be a constant looking upward to God. We should walk so habitually in His presence that even when we awake in the night, it would be the most natural thing for us to speak to Him in thanksgiving or petition.

CHAPTER 11

THE NEED FOR A GENERAL REVIVAL

If we are to pray correctly in such a time as this, many of our prayers should be for a general revival. If there was ever a need to cry to God in the words of the psalmist, "*Wilt thou not revive us again: that thy people may rejoice in thee?*" (Psalm 85:6), it is now. It is surely time for the Lord to work, for men have nullified His law. The voice of the Lord given in the written Word is made void both by the world and the church. This is not a time for discouragement: the man who believes in God and the Bible should never be discouraged. But it is a time for Jehovah Himself to step in and work. The intelligent Christian, the alert watchman on the walls of Zion, may well cry with the psalmist, "*It is time for thee, LORD, to work: for they have made void thy law*" (Psalm 119:126). The great need of the day is for a general revival. Let us consider first what a general revival is.

A revival is a time of quickening or impartation of life. As God alone can give life, a revival is a time when God visits His people. By the power of His Spirit, He imparts new life to them. Through them, He gives life to sinners "*dead in trespasses and sins*" (Ephesians 2:1). We have spiritual enthusiasm contrived by the cunning methods and hypnotic influence of the professional evangelist. But these are not revivals and are not needed. They are the devil's imitations of a revival. New life from God—that is a revival. A general revival is a time when this new life from God is not confined to scattered localities. It is general throughout Christendom and the earth.

The reason why a general revival is needed is that spiritual desolation and death affect everyone. They are not confined to any one country, though they may be more manifest in some countries than in others. They are found in mission fields as well as at home. We have had local revivals. The life-giving Spirit of God has breathed on this minister and that, this church and that, this community and that, but we sorely need a widespread, general revival.

Let us look at the results of a revival. These results are apparent in ministers of the church and in the unsaved.

REVIVAL IN MINISTERS

When ministers experience revival, they have a new love for souls. We ministers, as a rule, have an inadequate love for souls. We fall short of loving people as Jesus does or even Paul did. But when God visits His people, the hearts of ministers are heavily burdened for the unsaved. They go out in great longing for the salvation of their fellowmen. They forget their ambition to preach great sermons and to acquire fame; they simply long to see sinners brought to Christ.

Along with a renewed love for others, ministers receive a new love for and faith in God's Word. They cast away their doubts and criticisms of the Bible and start preaching it. They especially preach Christ crucified. Revivals make ministers who have become lax in their doctrines orthodox. A genuine, widespread revival is needed to set things right.

Revivals bring new liberty and power in preaching to ministers. It is no weeklong grind to prepare a sermon, and no nerve-consuming effort to preach it after it has been prepared. Preaching is a joy and refreshment. There is power in preaching during times of revival.

REVIVAL IN CHRISTIANS

The results of a revival in Christians generally are as noticeable as its results on the ministry. In times of revival, Christians come out from the world and live separated lives. Christians who have been amused with the world and its pleasures give them up. These things are found to be incompatible with increasing life and light.

IN TIMES OF REVIVAL, CHRISTIANS RECEIVE A NEW SPIRIT OF PRAYER. PRAYER MEETINGS ARE NO LONGER A DUTY BUT BECOME THE NECESSITY OF A HUNGRY, PERSISTENT HEART. PRIVATE PRAYER IS FOLLOWED WITH NEW ZEST.

In times of revival, Christians receive a new spirit of prayer. Prayer meetings are no longer a duty but become the necessity of a hungry, persistent heart. Private prayer is followed with new zest. The voice of earnest prayer to God is heard day and night. People no longer ask, "Does God answer prayer?" They know He does, and they besiege the throne of grace day and night.

In times of revival, Christians go to work to find lost souls. They do not go to meetings simply to enjoy themselves and get blessed. They go to meetings to watch for souls and to bring them to Christ. They talk to people on the street and in their homes. The cross of Christ, heaven, and hell become the subjects of conversation. Politics, the weather, news, and the latest novels are forgotten.

In times of revival, Christians have new joy in Christ. Life is joy, and new life is new joy. Revival days are glad days, days of heaven on earth.

In times of revival, Christians receive a new love for the Word of God. They want to study it day and night. Revivals are bad for bars and theaters, but they are good for bookstores and Bible publishers.

REVIVAL'S INFLUENCE ON THE UNSAVED

Revivals also have a decided influence on the unsaved world. First of all, they bring deep conviction of sin. Jesus said that when the Spirit comes, He convicts the world of sin. (See John 16:8.) Revival is a coming of the Holy Spirit; therefore, there must be a new conviction of sin, and there always is. If you see something that people call a revival and there is no conviction of sin, you may know immediately that it is not a revival. A lack of Holy Spirit conviction is a sure sign that there is no revival.

Revivals also bring conversion and regeneration. When God refreshes His people, He always converts sinners as well. The first result of Pentecost was new life and power to the one hundred and twenty disciples in the upper room. The second result was three thousand conversions in a single day. It is always so. I am constantly reading of revivals where Christians were greatly encouraged but there were no conversions. I have my doubts about that kind of revival. If Christians are truly refreshed, they will influence the unsaved by prayer, testimony, and persuasion. And there will be conversions.

WHY GENERAL REVIVAL IS NEEDED

We know what a general revival is and what it does. Let us now face the question of why it is needed at the present time. I think that the mere description of what it is and what it does shows why it is sorely needed. Let us look at some specific conditions that exist today that demonstrate the need for revival. In showing these conditions, one is likely to be called a pessimist. If facing the facts is pessimistic, I am willing to be called a pessimist. If in order to be an optimist one must shut his eyes and call black white, error truth, sin righteousness, and death life, I do not want to be an optimist. But I am an optimist all the same. Pointing out the real conditions will lead to better conditions.

Look again at the ministry. Many of us who profess to be orthodox ministers are practically nonbelievers. That is plain speech, but it is also indisputable fact. There is no essential difference between the teachings of the liberal Tom Paine and the teachings of some of our theological professors. The latter are not so blunt and honest about it. They phrase their beliefs in more elegant and studied sentences, but they mean the same. Much of the socalled new learning and higher criticism is simply Tom Paine's infidelity sugarcoated. A German professor once read a statement of some positions, then asked if they fairly represented the scholarly criticism of the day. When it was agreed that they did, he startled his audience by saying, "I am reading from Tom Paine's *Age of Reason.*"

There is little new in the higher criticism. Some of our future ministers are being educated under immoral professors. Being immature when they enter college or the seminary, they naturally come out nonbelievers in many cases. Then they go forth to poison the church.

Even when our ministers are orthodox—as, thank God, so very many are—they are not always people of prayer. How many modern ministers know what it is to wrestle in prayer, to spend a good share of a night in prayer? I do not know how many, but I do know that many do not.

Some ministers have no love for souls. How many preach because they must preach? How many preach because they feel that men everywhere are perishing, and by preaching they hope to save some? How many follow up their preaching, as Paul did, by beseeching men everywhere to be reconciled to God?

Perhaps enough has been said about us ministers. But it is evident that a revival is needed for our sakes. If not, some of us will have to stand before God overwhelmed with confusion in an awful day of reckoning that is surely coming.

Look now at the doctrinal state of the church. It is bad enough. Many do not believe in the whole Bible. They think that the book of Genesis is a myth, Jonah is an allegory, and even the miracles of the Son of God are questioned. The doctrine of prayer is old-fashioned, and the work of the Holy Spirit is scorned. Conversion is unnecessary, and hell is no longer believed in. Look at the fads and errors that have sprung up out of this loss of faith. Christian Science, Unitarianism, Spiritualism, Universalism, metaphysical healing, etc., a perfect pandemonium of the doctrines of the devil.

> PRAYERLESSNESS ABOUNDS AMONG CHURCH MEMBERS ON EVERY HAND. SOMEONE HAS SAID THAT CHRISTIANS, ON THE AVERAGE, DO NOT SPEND MORE THAN FIVE MINUTES A DAY IN PRAYER. NEGLECT OF THE WORD OF GOD GOES HAND IN HAND WITH NEGLECT OF PRAYER TO GOD.

Look at the spiritual state of the church. Worldliness is rampant among church members. Many church members are just as eager as any to become rich. They use the methods of the world in their efforts to accumulate wealth. And they hold on to it just as tightly once they have gotten it.

Prayerlessness abounds among church members on every hand. Someone has said that Christians, on the average, do not spend more than five minutes a day in prayer. Neglect of the Word of God goes hand in hand with neglect of prayer to God. Many Christians spend twice as much time everyday engrossed in the daily papers as they do bathing in the cleansing Word of God. How many Christians average an hour a day in Bible study?

A lack of generosity goes along with neglect of prayer and the Word of God. Churches are rapidly increasing in wealth, but the treasuries of missionary societies are empty. Christians do not average a dollar a year for missions. It is simply appalling.

Then, there is the increasing disregard for the Lord's Day. It is fast becoming a day of worldly pleasures, instead of a day of holy service. The Sunday newspaper with its mundane rambling and scandals has replaced the Bible. Recreational activities have replaced Sunday school and church services. Christians mingle with the world in all forms of questionable amusements. The young man or young woman who does not believe in wearing immodest clothing, participating in wild parties, and attending the theater with its ever increasing appeal to lewdness is considered an old fogy.

How small a proportion of our membership has really entered into fellowship with Jesus Christ in His burden for souls! Enough has been said of the spiritual state of the church. Now look at the state of the world. Note how few conversions there are. Here and there a church has a large number of new members joining by confession of faith, but these churches are rare. Where there are such new members, in very few cases are the conversions deep, thorough, and satisfactory.

There is lack of conviction of sin. Seldom are men overwhelmed with a sense of their awful guilt in dishonoring the Son of God. Sin is regarded as a misfortune, infirmity, or even as good in the making. Seldom is it considered an enormous wrong against a holy God.

Unbelief is rampant. Many regard it as a mark of intellectual superiority to reject the Bible as well as faith in God and immortality. It is often the only mark of intellectual superiority many possess. Perhaps that is the reason they cling to it so dearly.

UNBELIEF IS RAMPANT. MANY REGARD IT AS A MARK OF INTELLECTUAL SUPERIORITY TO REJECT THE BIBLE AS WELL AS FAITH IN GOD AND IMMORTALITY. IT IS OFTEN THE ONLY MARK OF INTELLECTUAL SUPERIORITY MANY POSSESS.

Hand in hand with this widespread atheism goes gross immorality, as has always been the case. Atheism and immorality are Siamese twins. They always exist and increase together. This prevailing immorality is found everywhere.

Look at the legalized adultery that we call divorce. Men marry one wife after another and are still admitted into good society, and women do likewise. Thousands of supposedly respectable men in America live with other men's wives. And there are thousands of supposedly respectable women living with other women's husbands.

This immorality is found in much modern theater. Many questionable characters of the stage rule the day. And the individuals who degrade themselves by appearing in such off-color plays are defended in the newspapers and welcomed by supposedly respectable people.

Much of our literature is rotten, but decent people will read bad books because they are popular. Art is often a mere covering for shameless indecency. Women are induced to cast modesty to the wind so that the artist may perfect his art and defile his morals.

Greed for money has become an obsession with the rich and poor. The multimillionaire will often sell his soul and trample the rights of his fellowmen in the hope of becoming a billionaire. The working man will often commit murder to increase the power of the union and keep up wages. Wars are waged and men shot down like dogs to improve commerce and to gain political prestige for unprincipled politicians who parade as statesmen.

The licentiousness of the day lifts its serpent head everywhere. You see it in the newspapers, on the billboards, in advertisements for cigars, shoes, bicycles, medicines, and everything else. You see it on the streets at night. You see it just outside the church door. You find it in the awful ghettos set apart for it in great cities. And it is crowding farther and farther up our business streets and into the residential portions of our cities. Alas! Every so often you find it, if you look closely, in supposedly respectable homes. Indeed it will be borne to your ears by the confessions of brokenhearted men and women. The moral condition of the world is disgusting, sickening, and appalling.

PRAY FOR REVIVAL

We need a revival—deep, widespread, and general—in the power of the Holy Spirit. It is either a general revival or the dissolution of the church, of the home, and of the state. A revival, new life from God, is the cure—the only cure. Revival will halt the awful tide of immorality and unbelief. Mere argument will not do it. But a wind from heaven, a new outpouring of the Holy Spirit, a true God-sent revival will. Atheism, higher criticism, Christian Science, Spiritualism, Universalism, all will go down before the outpouring of the Spirit of God. It was not discussion but the breath of God that banished nonbelievers of old to the limbo of forgetfulness. We need a new breath from God to send the current, radical non-Christians to keep those nonbelievers of old company. I believe that breath from God is coming.

The great need of today is a general revival. The need is clear. It allows no honest difference of opinion. What then must we do? Pray. Take up the psalmist's prayer: *"Wilt thou not revive us again: that thy people may rejoice in thee?"* (Psalm 85:6). Pray Ezekiel's prayer: *"Come from the four winds, O breath* [breath of God], *and breathe upon these slain, that they may live"* (Ezekiel 37:9). Hark, I hear a noise! Behold a shaking! I can almost feel the breeze on my cheek. I can almost see the great living army rising to their feet. Will we not pray and pray and pray until the Spirit comes, and God revives His people?

CHAPTER 12

PRAYER BEFORE AND DURING REVIVALS

No treatment of the subject of how to pray would be at all complete if it did not consider the place of prayer in revivals. The first great revival of Christian history had its origin on the human side in a ten-day prayer meeting. We read of that handful of disciples: *"These all continued with one accord in prayer and supplication"* (Acts 1:14). The result of that prayer meeting is in the second chapter of the Acts of the Apostles: *"They were all filled with the Holy Ghost, and began to speak with other tongues, as the Spirit gave them utterance"* (verse 4). Further in the chapter, we read that on *"the same day there were added unto them about three thousand souls"* (verse 41). This revival proved genuine and permanent. The converts *"continued steadfastly in the apostles' doctrine and fellowship, and in breaking of bread, and in prayers"* (verse 42). *"And the Lord added to the church daily such as should be saved"* (verse 47).

TESTIMONIES OF ANSWERED PRAYER

Every true revival from that day to this has had its earthly origin in prayer. The great revival under Jonathan Edwards in the eighteenth century began with his famous call to prayer. The marvelous work of grace among the Indians under Brainerd began in the days and nights that he spent before God in prayer for an anointing of *"power from on high"* (Luke 24:49) for this work.

A most remarkable and widespread display of God's reviving power was the revival in Rochester, New York, in 1830, under the labors of Charles G. Finney. It spread not only throughout the state but ultimately to Great Britain as well. Mr. Finney himself attributed the power of this work to the spirit of prayer that prevailed. He described it in his autobiography in the following words:

When I was on my way to Rochester, as we passed through a village, some thirty miles east of Rochester, a brother minister whom I knew, seeing me on the canal-boat, jumped aboard to have a little conversation with me, intending to ride but a little way and return. He, however, became interested in conversation, and upon finding where I was going, he made up his mind to keep on and go with me to Rochester. We had been there but a few days when this minister became so convicted that he could not help weeping aloud at one time as we passed along the street. The Lord gave him a powerful spirit of prayer, and his heart was broken. As he and I prayed together, I was struck with his faith in regard to what the Lord was going to do there. I recollect he would say, "Lord, I do not know how it is; but I seem to know that Thou art going to do a great work in this city." The spirit of prayer was poured out powerfully, so much so that some people stayed away from the public services to pray, being unable to restrain their feelings under preaching.

And here I must introduce the name of a man, whom I shall have occasion to mention frequently, Mr. Abel Clary. He was the son of a very excellent man, and an elder of the church where I was converted. He was converted in the same revival in which I was. He had been licensed to preach; but his spirit of prayer was such, he was so burdened with the souls of men, that he was not able to preach much, his whole time and strength being given to prayer. The burden of his soul would frequently be so great that he was unable to stand, and he would writhe and groan in agony. I was well acquainted with him, and knew something of the wonderful spirit of prayer that was upon him. He was a very silent man, as almost all are who have that powerful spirit of prayer.

The first I knew of his being in Rochester, a gentleman who lived about a mile west of the city called on me one day and asked me if I knew a Mr. Abel Clary, a minister. I told him that I knew him well.

"Well," he said, "he is at my house, and has been there for some time. I don't know what to think of him."

I said, "I have not seen him at any of our meetings."

"No," he replied, "he cannot go to meetings, he says. He prays nearly all the time, day and night, and in such agony of mind that I do not know what to make of it. Sometimes he cannot even stand on his knees, but will lie prostrate on the floor, and groan and pray in a manner that quite astonishes me."

I said to the brother, "I understand it: please keep still. It will come out right; he will surely prevail."

I knew at the time a considerable number of men who were exercised in the same way.... This Mr. Clary and many others among the men, and a large number of women, partook of the same spirit, and spent a great part of their time in prayer. Father Nash, as we called him who in several of my fields of labor came to me and aided me, was another of those men that had such a powerful spirit of prevailing prayer. This Mr. Clary continued in Rochester as long as I did, and did not leave it until after I had left. He never, that I could learn, appeared in public, but gave himself wholly to prayer.

I think it was the second Sabbath that I was at Auburn at this time, I observed in the congregation the solemn face of Mr. Clary. He looked as if he was borne down with an agony of prayer. Being well acquainted with him, and knowing the great gift of God that was upon him, the spirit of prayer, I was very glad to see him there. He sat in the pew with his brother, a doctor, who was also a professor of religion, but who had nothing by experience, I should think, of his brother Abel's great power with God.

At intermission, as soon as I came down from the pulpit, Mr. Clary and his brother met me at the pulpit stairs and invited me to go home with them and spend the intermission and get some refreshments. I did so.

After arriving at his house we were soon summoned to the dinner table. We gathered about the table, and Dr. Clary turned to his brother and said, "Brother Abel, will you ask the blessing?" Brother Abel bowed his head and began, audibly, to ask a blessing. He had uttered but a sentence or two when he broke instantly down, moved suddenly back from the table, and fled to his chamber. The doctor supposed he had been taken suddenly ill, and rose up and followed him. In a few moments he came down and said, "Mr. Finney, Brother Abel wants to see you."

Said I, "What ails him?"

Said he, "I do not know but he says you know. He appears in great distress, but I think it is the state of his mind."

I understood it in a moment, and went to his room. He lay groaning upon the bed, the Spirit making intercession for him, and in him, with groanings that could not be uttered. I had barely entered the room, when he made out to say, "Pray, Brother Finney." I knelt down and helped him in prayer, by leading his soul out for the conversion of sinners. I continued to pray until his distress passed away, and then I returned to the dinner table.

I understood that this was the voice of God. I saw the Spirit of prayer was upon him, and I felt His influence upon myself, and took it for granted that the work would move on powerfully. It did so. The pastor told me afterward that he found that in the six weeks that I was there, five hundred souls had been converted.

PERSISTENT PRAYER RESULTS

Mr. Finney in his lectures on revivals told of other remarkable awakenings in answer to the prayers of God's people. He said,

A clergyman…told me of a revival among his people, which commenced with a zealous and devoted woman in the church. She became anxious about sinners, and went to praying for them; she prayed, and her distress increased; and she finally came to her minister, and talked with him, and asked him to appoint an anxious meeting, for she felt that one was needed. The minister put her off, for he felt nothing of it. The next week she came again, and besought him to appoint an anxious meeting; she knew there would be somebody to come, for she felt as if God was going to pour out His Spirit. He put her off again. And finally she said to him, "If you do not appoint an anxious meeting I shall die, for there is certainly going to be a revival." The next Sabbath he appointed a meeting, and said that if there were any who wished to converse with him about the salvation of their souls, he would meet them on such an evening. He did not know of one, but when he went to the place, to his astonishment he found a large number of anxious inquirers.

In still another place, Finney said,

The first ray of light that broke in upon the midnight which rested on the churches in Oneida county, in the fall of 1825, was from a woman in feeble health, who I believe had never been in a powerful revival. Her soul was exercised about sinners. She was in agony for the land. She did not know what ailed her, but she kept praying more and more, till it seemed as if her agony would destroy her body. At length she became full of joy and exclaimed, "God has come! God has come! There is no mistake about it, the work is begun, and is going over all the region!" And sure enough, the work began, and her family was almost all converted, and the work spread all over that part of the country.

The great revival of 1857 in the United States began in prayer and was carried on by prayer more than by anything else. Dr. Cuyler in an article in a religious newspaper some years ago said,

Most revivals have humble beginnings, and the fire starts in a few warm hearts. Never despise the day of small things. During all my own long ministry, nearly every work of grace has had a similar beginning. One commenced in a meeting gathered at a few hours' notice in a private house. Another commenced in a group gathered for Bible study by Mr. Moody in our mission chapel. Still another—the most powerful of all—was kindled on a bitter January evening at a meeting of young Christians under my roof. That profound Christian, Dr. Thomas H. Skinner of the Union Theological Seminary, once gave me an account of a remarkable coming together of three earnest men in his study when he was the pastor of the Arch Street church in Philadelphia. They wrestled in prayer. They made a clean breast in confession of sin, and humbled themselves before God. One and another church officer came in and joined them. The heaven-kindled flame soon spread through the whole congregation in one of the most powerful revivals ever known in that city.

PRAYER KNOWS NO BOUNDARIES

In the early part of the sixteenth century, there was a great religious awakening in Ulster, Ireland. The lands of the rebel chiefs, which had been forfeited to the British crown, were settled by a class of colonists who were governed by a spirit of wild adventure. Authentic righteousness was rare. Seven ministers, five from Scotland and two from England, settled in that country, the earliest arrivals being in 1613. A contemporary of one of these ministers named Blair recorded, "He spent many days and nights in prayer, alone and with others, and was vouchsafed great intimacy with God." Mr. James Glendenning, a man of very meager natural gifts, was a man similarly minded in regard to prayer. The work began under this man Glendenning. The historian of the time said,

> He was a man who never would have been chosen by a wise assembly of ministers, nor sent to begin a reformation in this land. Yet this was the Lord's choice to begin with him the admirable work of God which I mention on purpose that all may see how the glory is only the Lord's in making a holy nation in this profane land, and that it was *"not by might, nor by power, but by my spirit, saith the* Lord *of hosts"* (Zechariah 4:6).

In his preaching at Oldstone, multitudes of hearers felt great anxiety and terror of conscience. They looked on themselves as altogether lost and damned and cried out, "Men and women, what will we do to be saved?" They were stricken and became faint by the power of His Word. In one day, a dozen were carried out of doors as dead. These were not cowards, but some of the boldest spirits of the neighborhood, "some who had formerly feared not with their swords to put a whole market town into a fray." Concerning one of them, the historian wrote, "I have heard one of them, then a mighty strong man, now a mighty Christian, say that his end in coming into church was to consult with his companions how to work some mischief."

This work spread throughout the whole country of Ireland. By the year 1626, a monthly concert of prayer was held in Antrim. The work spread beyond the bounds of Down and Antrim to the churches of the neighboring counties. The spiritual interest became so great that Christians would come thirty or forty miles to the communions. They would continue from the time they came until they returned without wearying or making use of sleep. Many of them neither ate not drank, and yet some of them professed that they "went away most fresh and vigorous, their souls so filled with the sense of God." This revival changed the whole character of northern Ireland.

Another great awakening in Ireland in 1859 had a somewhat similar origin. By many who were unaware, it was thought that this marvelous work came without warning and preparation. But Rev. William Gibson, moderator of the General Assembly of the Presbyterian church in Ireland in 1860, in his history of the awakening, told how there had been two years of preparation. There had been constant discussion in the General Assembly of the low state of spiritual fervor and the need of a revival. There had been special sessions for prayer. Finally, four young men who became leaders in the origin of the great work began to meet together in an old schoolhouse. Around the spring of 1858, a work of power began to manifest itself. It spread from town to town, from county to county. The congregations became too large for the buildings, and the meetings were held outside. They were often attended by many thousands of people. Many hundreds of people were frequently convicted of sin in a single meeting. In some places, the criminal courts and jails were closed for lack of occupation. There were manifestations of the Holy Spirit's power of a most remarkable character. This clearly proves that the Holy Spirit is as ready to work today as in apostolic days. He will do so when ministers and Christians really believe in Him and begin to prepare the way by prayer.

Mr. Moody's wonderful work in England, Scotland, and Ireland, then afterward in America, originated in prayer. Moody made little impression until men and women began to cry to God. Indeed, his going to England at all was in answer to the persistent cries to God by a bedridden saint. While the spirit of prayer continued, the revival grew in strength. But in the course of time, less and less was made of prayer, and the work fell off in power. One of the great secrets of the superficiality and unreality of many of our modern, so-called revivals is that more dependence is put on man's machinery than on God's power. His power must be sought and obtained by earnest, persistent, believing prayer. We live in a day characterized by the multiplication of man's machinery and the decrease of God's power. The great cry of our day is work, new organizations, new methods, and new machinery. The great need of our day is prayer.

CHURCH, WAKE UP!

It was a masterstroke of Satan when he got the church to so generally lay aside this mighty weapon of prayer. Satan is perfectly willing that the church multiply its organizations and contrive machinery for the conquest of the world for Christ if it will only give up praying. He laughs as he looks at the church today and says to himself, "You can have your Sunday schools and your Young People's Societies. Enjoy your Young Men's and Women's Christian Associations. Continue your institutional churches, your industrial schools, and your Boys' Brigades. Worship with your grand choirs, your fine organs, your brilliant preachers, and your revival efforts, too. But don't bring the power of almighty God into them by earnest, persistent, believing, mighty prayer." Prayer could work as marvelously today as it ever could, if the church would only take up the call.

> THERE IS EVERY INDICATION OF THE COMING OF A MIGHTY, WIDESPREAD REVIVAL. THERE IS EVERY REASON WHY, IF A REVIVAL SHOULD COME IN ANY COUNTRY AT THIS TIME, IT SHOULD BE MORE WIDESPREAD IN ITS EXTENT THAN ANY REVIVAL OF HISTORY. A TRUE FIRE OF GOD KINDLED IN AMERICA WOULD SOON SPREAD TO THE UTTERMOST PARTS OF THE EARTH.

There seem to be increasing signs that the church is awaking to this fact. God is laying a burden of prayer on individual ministers and churches like they have never known before. Less dependence is being placed on human instrumentality and more on God. Ministers are crying to God day and night for power. Churches and groups are meeting together in the early morning and the late night hours crying to God for the *"latter rain"* (Deuteronomy 11:14). There is every indication of the coming of a mighty, widespread revival. There is every reason why, if a revival should come in any country at this time, it should be more widespread in its extent than any revival of history. There is the closest and swiftest communication among all parts of the world. A true fire of God kindled in America would soon spread to the uttermost parts of the earth. The only thing needed to bring this fire is prayer.

It is not necessary that the whole church begins praying at first. Great revivals always begin in the hearts of a few men and women whom God arouses by His Spirit to believe in Him as a living God. They believe He is a God who answers prayer. He lays a burden on their hearts from which no rest can be found except in persistent crying to God.

May God use this book to arouse many others to pray so that the greatly needed revival will come, and come quickly. Let us pray!

HOW TO STUDY THE BIBLE

INTRODUCTION

The Bible contains golden nuggets of truth, and anyone willing to dig for biblical truth is certain to find it.

Those reading this book for the first time must not become frightened at the elaborate methods I will suggest. They are not difficult. Their fruitfulness has been tested with those who have varying degrees of education, and the results have been found to be practical. As you use the methods I will recommend, you will soon find your ability to study the Bible rapidly increasing, until you will accomplish more in fifteen minutes than you once could in an hour.

Although the Bible is read much, comparatively, it is studied little. The methods you will learn are the same methods being used in highly technical fields, such as science and medicine. First, you will make a careful analysis of the facts. Then, you will learn how to classify those facts. While we cannot all be students of technology, we can all be profound students of Scripture. No other book than the Bible offers the opportunity for intellectual development by its study. People who have studied few books besides the Scriptures have astonished and amazed scholars and theologians.

The truths you will find as you study Scripture will far transcend any other study in inspiration, helpfulness, and practical value. They will, in fact, become life-changing.

CHAPTER 1

CONDITIONS FOR PROFITABLE BIBLE STUDY

While you will be learning profitable methods for Bible study, there is something more important than the best procedures. The secret lies in meeting certain fundamental conditions before you begin to study God's Word. If you meet these conditions, you will get more out of the Bible, even while pursuing the poorest methods, than the one who does not meet them while he pursues the best methods. What you will need is far deeper than a new and better technique.

OBTAINING SPIRITUAL UNDERSTANDING

The most essential of these conditions is that *"ye must be born again"* (John 3:7). The Bible is a spiritual book. It combines spiritual concepts with spiritual words. Only a spiritual man can understand its deepest and most precious teachings. *"The natural man receiveth not the things of the Spirit of God: for they are foolishness unto him: neither can he know them, because they are spiritually discerned"* (1 Corinthians 2:14).

Spiritual discernment can be obtained in only one way: by being born again—*"Except a man be born again, he cannot see the kingdom of God"* (John 3:3). No mere knowledge of the human languages in which the Bible was written, however extensive and accurate it may be, will qualify one to understand and appreciate the Bible. One must comprehend the divine language in which it was written as well as the language of the Holy Spirit.

A person who understands the language of the Holy Spirit but who does not understand a word of Greek, Hebrew, or Aramaic will get more out of the Bible than one who knows all about ancient languages but is not born again. Many ordinary men and women who possess no knowledge of the original languages in which the Bible was written have a knowledge of the real contents of the Bible. Their understanding of its actual teaching and its depth, fullness, and beauty far surpasses that of many learned professors in theological seminaries.

One of the greatest follies today is to allow an unregenerate person to teach the Bible. It would be just as unreasonable to allow someone to teach art because he had an accurate, technical knowledge of paints. An aesthetic sense is required to make a person a competent art teacher. Likewise, it requires spiritual sense to make a person a competent Bible teacher.

One who has aesthetic discernment but little or no technical knowledge of paint would be a far more competent critic of works of art than one who has extensive technical knowledge of paint but no aesthetic discernment. Similarly, the person who has no technical knowledge of biblical languages but who has spiritual discernment is a far more competent critic of the Bible than the one who has a rare knowledge of Greek and Hebrew but no spiritual discernment.

It is unfortunate that more emphasis is often placed on a knowledge of Greek and Hebrew in training for the ministry than is placed on the spiritual life and its consequent spiritual discernment. Unregenerate people should not be forbidden to study the Bible because the Word of God is the instrument the Holy Spirit uses in the new birth. (See 1 Peter 1:23; James 1:18.) But it should be distinctly understood that while there are teachings in the Bible that the natural man can understand, its most distinctive, characteristic teachings are beyond his grasp. Its highest beauties belong to a world in which he has no vision.

The first fundamental condition for profitable Bible study, then, is "*Ye must be born again*" (John 3:7). You cannot study the Bible to the greatest profit if you have not been born again. Its best treasures are sealed to you.

GAINING A SPIRITUAL APPETITE

The second condition for profitable study is to have a love for the Bible. A person who eats with an appetite will get far more good out of his meal than one who eats from a sense of duty. A student of the Bible should be able to say with Job, "*I have esteemed the words of his mouth more than my necessary food*" (Job 23:12), or with Jeremiah, "*Thy words were found, and I did eat them; and thy word was unto me the joy and rejoicing of mine heart: for I am called by thy name, O LORD God of hosts"* (Jeremiah 15:16).

Many come to the table God has spread in His Word with no appetite for spiritual food. Instead of getting their fill of the feast God has prepared, they grumble about everything. Spiritual indigestion results from much of the modern criticism of the Bible.

But how can one acquire a love for the Bible? First of all, by being born again. Where there is life, there is likely to be appetite. A dead man never hungers. But going beyond this, the more there is of vitality, the more there is of hunger. Abounding life means abounding hunger for the Word.

Study of the Word stimulates love for the Word. I remember when I had more appetite for books about the Bible than I had for the Bible itself; but with increasing study, there has come increasing love for the Book. Bearing in mind who the Author of the Book is, what its purpose is, what its power is, and what the riches of its contents are will go far toward stimulating a love and appetite for the Book.

DIGGING FOR TREASURES

The third condition is a willingness to work hard. Solomon gave a graphic picture of the Bible student who receives the most profit from his study:

> *My son, if thou wilt receive my words, and hide my commandments with thee; so that you incline thine ear unto wisdom, and apply thine heart to understanding; yea, if thou criest after knowledge, and liftest up thy voice for understanding; if thou seekest her as silver, and searchest for her as for hid treasures; shalt thou understand the fear of the LORD, and find the knowledge of God.* (Proverbs 2:1–5)

SEEKING FOR SILVER AND SEARCHING FOR HIDDEN TREASURE MEAN HARD WORK, AND THE ONE WHO WISHES TO GET NOT ONLY THE SILVER BUT ALSO THE GOLD OUT OF THE BIBLE MUST MAKE UP HIS MIND TO DIG.

Seeking for silver and searching for hidden treasure mean hard work, and the one who wishes to get not only the silver but also the gold out of the Bible must make up his mind to dig. It is not glancing at the Word but studying the Word, meditating on the Word, and pondering the Word that will bring the richest yield.

The reason many people get so little out of their Bible reading is simply that they are not willing to think. Intellectual laziness lies at the heart of a large percent of fruitless Bible reading. People are constantly crying for new methods of Bible study, but what many of them want is simply some method of Bible study where they can get the most without much work.

If someone could tell lazy Christians some method of Bible study whereby they could use the sleepiest ten minutes of the day, just before they go to bed, for Bible study and get the most profit that God intends, that would be what they desire. But it can't be done. We must be willing to work and work hard if we wish to dig out the treasures of infinite wisdom, knowledge, and blessing that He has stored up in His Word.

A business friend once asked me in a hurried call to tell him "in a word" how to study his Bible. I replied, "Think." The psalmist pronounced that the man who *"meditate[s] day and night"* *"in the law of the Lord"* is *"blessed"* (Psalm 1:1–2). The Lord commanded Joshua to *"meditate day and night"* and assured him that as a result of this meditation, *"thou shalt make thy way prosperous, and then thou shalt have good success"* (Joshua 1:8). In this way alone can one study the Bible to the greatest profit.

One pound of beef well-chewed, digested, and assimilated will give more strength than tons of beef merely glanced at; and one verse of Scripture chewed, digested, and assimilated will give more strength than whole chapters simply skimmed. Weigh every word you read in the Bible. Look at it. Turn it over and over. The most familiar passages take on new meaning in this way. Spend fifteen minutes on each word in Psalm 23:1 or Philippians 4:19, and see if it is not so.

FINDING THE TREASURE'S KEYS

The fourth condition is a will wholly surrendered to God: *"If any man will do his will, he shall know of the doctrine"* (John 7:17). A surrendered will gives that clearness of spiritual vision necessary to understand God's

Book. Many of the difficulties and obscurities of the Bible arise simply because the will of the student is not surrendered to the will of the Author of the Book.

It is remarkable how clear, simple, and beautiful passages that once puzzled us become when we are brought to that place where we say to God, "I surrender my will unconditionally to Yours. I have no will but Yours. Teach me Your will." A surrendered will does more than a university education to make the Bible an open book. It is simply impossible to get the most profit out of your Bible study until you surrender your will to God. You must be very definite about this.

Many will say, "Oh, yes, my will is surrendered to God," but it is not. They have never gone alone with God and said intelligently and definitely to Him, "O God, I here and now give myself to You, for You to command me, lead me, shape me, send me, and do with me absolutely as You will." Such an act is a wonderful key to unlock the treasure-house of God's Word. The Bible becomes a new Book when a person surrenders to God. Doing this brought a complete transformation in my own theology, life, and ministry.

USE IT OR LOSE IT

The fifth condition is very closely related to the fourth. The student of the Bible who desires to receive the greatest profit out of his studies must be obedient to its teachings as soon as he sees them. It was good advice James gave to early Christians and to us: *"Be ye doers of the word, and not hearers only, deceiving your own selves"* (James 1:22).

Many who consider themselves Bible students are deceiving themselves in this way today. They see what the Bible teaches, but they do not do it; soon, they lose their power to see it. Truth obeyed leads to more truth. Truth disobeyed destroys the capacity for discovering truth.

There must be not only a general surrender of the will but also a specific, practical obedience to each new word of God discovered. In no place is the law more joyously certain on the one hand and more sternly inexorable on the other than in the matter of using or refusing the truth revealed in the Bible: *"Unto every one that hath shall be given, and he shall have abundance: but from him that hath not shall be taken away even that which he hath"* (Matthew 25:29). Use and you get more; refuse and you lose all.

Do not study the Bible for the mere gratification of intellectual curiosity but to find out how to live and how to please God. Whatever duty you find commanded in the Bible, do it at once. Whatever good you see in any Bible character, imitate it immediately. Whatever mistake you note in the actions of Bible men and women, scrutinize your own life to see if you are making the same mistake; if you find you are, correct it immediately.

James compared the Bible to a mirror. (See James 1:23–24.) The chief purpose of a mirror is to show you if anything is out of place about you. If you find there is, you can set it right. Use the Bible in that way.

You already see that obeying the truth will solve the enigmas in the verses you do not yet understand. Disobeying the truth darkens the whole world of truth. This is the secret of much of the skepticism and error of the day. People saw the truth but did not do it, and now it is gone.

I once knew a bright and promising young minister who made rapid advancement in the truth. One day, however, he said to his wife, "It's nice to believe this truth, but we do not need to speak so much about it." He began to hide his testimony. Not long after this, his wife died, and he began to drift. The Bible became a sealed book to him. His faith reeled, and he publicly renounced his belief in the fundamental truths of the Bible. He seemed to lose his grip even on the doctrine of immortality. What was the cause of it all? Truth flees when it is not lived and stood for. That man was admired by many and applauded by some, but light gave place to darkness in his soul.

COME AS A CHILD

The sixth condition is a childlike mind. God reveals His deepest truths to babes. No time more than our own needs to take to heart the words of Jesus: *"I thank thee, O Father, Lord of heaven and earth, because thou hast hid these things from the wise and prudent, and hast revealed them unto babes"* (Matthew 11:25).

How can we be babes if God is to reveal His truth to us, and we are to understand His Word? By having a childlike spirit. A child is not full of his own wisdom. He recognizes his ignorance and is ready to be taught. He does not oppose his own notions and ideas to those of his teachers.

It is in this spirit that we should come to the Bible if we are to get the most profit out of our study. Do not come to the Bible seeking confirmation for your own ideas. Come rather to find out what God's ideas are as He has revealed them. Do not come to find confirmation for your own opinions but to be taught what God may be pleased to teach. If a person comes to the Bible just to find his own ideas taught there, he will find them. But if he comes, recognizing his own ignorance just as a little child seeks to be taught, he will find something infinitely better than his own ideas; he will find the mind of God.

Thus, we see why many people cannot see things that are plainly taught in the Bible. They are so full of their own ideas that there is no room left for what the Bible actually teaches.

An illustration of this is given in the lives of the apostles at one stage in their training. In Mark 9:31, we read, *"For he taught his disciples, and said unto them, The Son of man is delivered into the hands of men, and they shall kill him; and after that he is killed, he shall rise the third day."* Now this is as plain and definite as language can make it, but it was utterly contrary to the apostles' ideas of what would happen to Christ.

> IF A PERSON COMES TO THE BIBLE JUST TO FIND HIS OWN IDEAS TAUGHT THERE, HE WILL FIND THEM. BUT IF HE COMES, RECOGNIZING HIS OWN IGNORANCE JUST AS A LITTLE CHILD SEEKS TO BE TAUGHT, HE WILL FIND SOMETHING INFINITELY BETTER THAN HIS OWN IDEAS; HE WILL FIND THE MIND OF GOD.

We read in the next verse: *"They understood not that saying, and were afraid to ask him"* (verse 32). Is this any different than our own inability to comprehend plain statements in the Bible when they run counter to our preconceived notions?

You must come to Christ like a child to be taught what to believe and do, rather than coming as a full-grown person who already knows it all and must find some interpretations of Christ's words that will fit into his mature and infallible philosophy. Many people are so full of unbiblical theology that it takes a lifetime to get rid of it and understand the clear teaching of the Bible. "Oh, what can this verse mean?" many bewildered individuals cry. It means what it clearly says. But these people are not after the meaning God has clearly put into it, but the meaning they can, by some ingenious tricks of explanation, twist to make fit into their own interpretations.

Don't come to the Bible to find out what you can make it mean but to find out what God intended it to mean. People often miss the real truth of a verse by saying, "But that can be interpreted this way." Oh, yes, so it can, but is that the way God intended it to be interpreted?

We all need to pray, "O, God, make me like a little child. Empty me of my own notions. Teach me Your own mind. Make me ready to receive all that You have to say, no matter how contrary it is to what I have thought before." How the Bible opens up to one who approaches it in this way! How it closes to the fool who thinks he knows everything and imagines he can give points to Peter, Paul, and even to God Himself!

I was once talking with a ministerial friend about what seemed to be the clear teaching of a certain passage. "Yes," he replied, "but that doesn't agree with my philosophy." This man was sincere, yet he did not have the childlike spirit essential for productive Bible study. We have reached an important point in Bible study when we realize that an infinite God knows more than we, that our highest wisdom is less than the knowledge of the most ignorant babe compared with His, and that we must come to Him to be taught as children.

We are not to argue with Him. But we so easily and so constantly forget this point that every time we open our Bibles, we should bow humbly before God and say, "Father, I am but a child; please teach me."

BELIEVING GOD'S WORD

The seventh condition of studying the Bible for the greatest profit is that we study it as the Word of God. The apostle Paul, in writing to the Thessalonians, thanked God *"without ceasing"* that when they received the Word of God, they *"received it not as the word of men, but as it is in truth, the word of God"* (1 Thessalonians 2:13). Paul thanked God for that, and so may we thank God when we get to the place where we receive the Word of God as *the* Word of God.

He who does not believe the Bible is the Word of God should be encouraged to study it. Once I doubted that the Bible was the Word of God, but the firm confidence that I have today that the Bible is the Word of God has come more from the study of the Book itself than from anything else. Those who doubt it are more usually those who study about the Book rather than those who dig into the actual teachings of the Book.

Studying the Bible as the Word of God involves four things. First, it involves the unquestioning acceptance of its teachings when they are definitely understood, even when they may appear unreasonable or impossible. Reason demands that we submit our judgment to the statements of infinite wisdom. Nothing is more irrational than rationalism. It makes finite wisdom the test of infinite wisdom and submits the teachings of God's omniscience to the approval of man's judgment. Conceit says, "This cannot be true, even though God says it, for it does not approve itself to my reason." *"O man, who art thou that repliest against God?"* (Romans 9:20).

Real human wisdom, when it finds infinite wisdom, bows before it and says, "Speak what You will and I will believe." When we have once become convinced that the Bible is God's Word, its teachings must be the end of all controversy and discussion. A "Thus says the Lord" will settle every question. Yet many who profess to believe that the Bible is the Word of God will shake their heads and say, "Yes, but I think so and so," or "Doctor _____ or Professor _____ or our church doesn't teach it that way." There is little advantage to that sort of study.

Second, studying the Bible as the Word of God involves absolute reliance on all its promises in all their length and breadth. The person who studies the Bible as the Word of God will not discount any one of its promises one iota. A student who studies the Bible as the Word of God will say, "God who cannot lie has promised," and he will not try to make God a liar by trying to make one of His promises mean less than it says. (See 1 John 5:10.) The one who studies the Bible as the Word of God will be on the lookout for promises. As soon as he finds one, he should seek to discover what it means and then place his entire trust on its full meaning.

This is one of the secrets of profitable Bible study. Hunt for promises and appropriate them as fast as you find them by meeting the conditions and risking all upon them. This is the way to make all the fullness of God's blessing your own. This is the key to all the treasures of God's grace. Happy is the one who has learned to study the Bible as God's Word and is ready to claim for himself every new promise as it appears and to risk everything on it.

> HAPPY IS THE ONE WHO HAS LEARNED TO STUDY THE BIBLE AS GOD'S WORD AND IS READY TO CLAIM FOR HIMSELF EVERY NEW PROMISE AS IT APPEARS AND TO RISK EVERYTHING ON IT.

Next, studying the Bible as the Word of God involves prompt obedience to its every precept. Obedience may seem hard and impossible; but God has commanded it, and you have nothing to do but to obey and leave the results with God. To get results from your Bible study, resolve that from this time on, you will claim every clear promise and obey every plain command. When the meaning of promises and commands is not yet clear, try to discern their meaning immediately.

Finally, studying the Bible as the Word of God involves studying it in God's presence. When you read a verse of Scripture, hear the voice of the living God speaking directly to you in these written words. There is new power and attractiveness in the Bible when you have learned to hear a living, present Person—God our Father—talking directly to you in these words.

One of the most fascinating and inspiring statements in the Bible is *"Enoch walked with God"* (Genesis 5:24). We can have God's glorious companionship any moment we please by simply opening His Word and letting the living, ever present God speak to us through it. With what holy awe and strange and unutterable joy one studies the Bible if he studies it in this way! It is heaven come down to earth.

THE KEY TO UNDERSTANDING

The last condition for profitable Bible study is prayerfulness. The psalmist prayed, *"Open thou mine eyes, that I may behold wondrous things out of thy law"* (Psalm 119:18). Everyone who desires productive study needs to offer a similar prayer each time he undertakes to study the Word.

A few keys open many treasure chests of prayer. A few clues unravel many difficulties. A few microscopes disclose many beauties hidden from the eye of the ordinary observer. What new light often shines from familiar texts as you bend over them in prayer!

I believe in studying the Bible many times on your knees. When you read an entire book through on your knees—and this is easily done—that book takes on a new meaning and becomes a new book. You should never open the Bible without at least lifting your heart to God in silent prayer that He will interpret it and illumine its pages by the light of His Spirit. It is a rare privilege to study any book under the immediate guidance and instruction of the author, and this is the privilege of us all in studying the Bible.

When you come to a passage that is difficult to understand or interpret, instead of giving up or rushing to some learned friend or some commentary, lay that passage before God and ask Him to explain it. Plead God's promise *"If any of you lack wisdom, let him ask of God, that giveth to all men liberally, and upbraideth not; and it shall be given him let him ask in faith, nothing wavering"* (James 1:5–6).

Harry Morehouse, one of the most remarkable Bible scholars among unlearned men, used to say that whenever he came to a passage in the Bible that he could not understand, he would search through the Bible for another passage that threw light on it and place it before God in prayer. He said he had never found a passage that did not yield to this treatment.

Some years ago, I took a tour of Switzerland with a friend, visiting some of the more famous caves. One day, the country letter carrier stopped us and asked if we would like to see a cave of rare beauty and interest away from the beaten tracks of travel. Of course, we said yes. He led us through the woods and underbrush to the mouth of the cave. As we entered, all was dark and eerie. He expounded greatly on the beauty of the cave, telling us of altars and fantastic formations, but we could see absolutely nothing. Now and then he uttered a note to warn us to be careful since near our feet lay a gulf whose bottom had never been discovered. We began to fear that we might be the first discoverers of its depth.

There was nothing pleasant about the whole affair. But as soon as a magnesium taper was lit, all became different. Stalagmites rose from the floor to meet the stalactites descending from the ceiling. The great altar of nature that has been ascribed to the skill of ancient worshippers, and the beautiful and fantastic formations on every hand all glistened in fairylike beauty in the brilliant light.

I have often thought it was like a passage of Scripture. Others tell you of its beauty, but you cannot see it. It looks dark, intricate, forbidding, and dangerous; but when God's own light is kindled there by prayer, how different it all becomes in an instant! You see a beauty that language cannot express. Only those who have stood there in the same light can appreciate it. He who desires to understand and love the Bible must pray much. Prayer will do more than a college education to make the Bible an open and glorious book.

CHAPTER 2

INDIVIDUAL BOOK STUDY

The first method of Bible study that we will consider is the study of individual books. This method of study is the most thorough and the most difficult, but the one that yields the most permanent results. We examine it first because, in my opinion, it should occupy the greater portion of our time.

HOW TO BEGIN

The first step is selecting the correct book of the Bible to study. If you make an unfortunate selection, you may become discouraged and give up a method of study that might have been most fruitful.

For your first book study, choose a short book. Choosing a long book to begin with leads to discouragement. The average student will give up before the final results are reached.

Choose a comparatively easy book. Some books of the Bible are harder to understand than others. You may want to meet and overcome these later, but they are not recommended work for a beginner. When you are more familiar with Scripture as a whole, then you can tackle these books successfully and satisfactorily. You will find yourself floundering if you begin the more difficult books too soon.

The first epistle of Peter is an exceedingly precious book, but a few of the most difficult passages in the Bible are in it. If it were not for these hard passages, it would be a good book to recommend to the beginner. In view of these difficulties, it is not wise to undertake it until later.

Choose a book that is rich enough in its teaching to illustrate the advantage of this method of study and thus give a keen appetite for further studies of the same kind. Once you have gone through one reasonably large book by the method of study about to be described, you will have an eagerness that will encourage you to find time for further studies.

A book that meets all the conditions stated is the first epistle of Paul to the Thessalonians. It is quite short, has no great difficulties in interpretation, and is exceedingly rich in its teaching. It has the further advantage of being the first of the Pauline Epistles. The first epistle of John is also a good book to begin with and is not difficult.

POSSESSING THE TRUTHS

The second step is to master the general contents of the book. The method is very simple. It consists in merely reading the book through without stopping, then reading it through again and again, say a dozen times in all, at a single sitting. To one who has never tried this, it does not seem as if that would amount to much. But any thoughtful man who has ever tried it will tell you quite differently.

It is simply wonderful how a book takes on new meaning and beauty. It begins to open up. New relationships between different parts of the book begin to disclose themselves. Fascinating lines of thought running through the book appear. The book is grasped as a whole, and a foundation is laid for an intelligent study of those parts in detail.

Rev. James M. Gray of Boston, a prominent teacher and a great lover of the Bible, said that for many years of his ministry he had "an inadequate and unsatisfactory knowledge of the Bible." The first practical idea he received in the study of the Bible was from a layman. The brother possessed an unusual serenity and joy in his Christian experience, which he attributed to his reading of the letter to the Ephesians.

Gray asked him how he read it. The man said that he had taken a pocket copy of the Scriptures into the woods one Sunday afternoon and read Ephesians through at a single sitting, repeating the process a dozen times before stopping. When he arose, he had gained possession of the epistle or, rather, its wondrous truths had gained possession of him. This was the secret, simple as it was, that Gray had been waiting and praying for. From that time on, he studied his Bible in this way, and it became a new Book to him.

PRACTICAL PRINCIPLES FOR STUDY

The third step is to prepare an introduction to the book. Write down at the top of separate sheets of paper or cards the following questions:

ote this book?

was it written?

..nere did the author write it?

+ When did he write it?

+ What was the occasion of his writing?

+ What was the purpose for which he wrote?

+ What were the circumstances of the author when he wrote?

+ What were the circumstances of those to whom he wrote?

+ What glimpses does the book give into the life and character of the author?

+ What are the leading ideas of the book?

+ What is the central truth of the book?

+ What are the characteristics of the book?

Having prepared your sheets of paper with these headings, lay them side by side on your study table. Go through the book slowly, and as you come to an answer to any one of these questions, write it down on the appropriate sheet of paper. It may be necessary to go through the book several times to do the work thoroughly and satisfactorily, but you will be amply rewarded. After you have completed this process, and not until then, it would be good to refer to commentaries to compare your results with those reached by others.

The introduction you prepare for yourself will be worth many times more to you than anything you can gain from the research of others. Your study will be a rare education of the facilities of perception, comparison, and reasoning.

SEEING THE BIG PICTURE

Sometimes the answers to our questions will be found in a related book. For example, if you are studying one of the Pauline Epistles, the answers to your questions may be found in the Acts of the Apostles or in another letter. Of course, all the questions given will not apply to every book in the Bible.

If you are not willing to give the time and effort necessary, this introductory work can be omitted but only at a great sacrifice. Single passages in an epistle can never be correctly understood unless we know to whom they were written. Much false interpretation of the Bible arises from taking a local application and applying it as universal authority. Also, false interpretations often arise from applying to the unbeliever what was intended for the believer.

> MUCH FALSE INTERPRETATION OF THE BIBLE ARISES FROM TAKING A LOCAL APPLICATION AND APPLYING IT AS UNIVERSAL AUTHORITY. ALSO, FALSE INTERPRETATIONS OFTEN ARISE FROM APPLYING TO THE UNBELIEVER WHAT WAS INTENDED FOR THE BELIEVER.

Note the occasion of the writing. It will clear up the meaning of a passage that would otherwise be obscure. Bearing in mind the circumstances of the author as he wrote will frequently give new force to his words. The jubilant epistle to the Philippians contains repeated phrases, such as *"rejoice in the Lord"* (Philippians 3:1; 4:4), *"trust in the Lord"* (Philippians 2:19, 24), and *"be careful for nothing"* (Philippians 4:6). Remember that these words were written by a prisoner awaiting a possible sentence of death, and then they will become more meaningful to you.

If you will remember the main purpose for which a book was written, it will help you to interpret its incidental exhortations in their proper relationship. In fact, the answers to all the questions will be valuable in all the work that follows, as well as valuable in themselves.

DIVIDE AND CONQUER

The fourth step is to divide the book into its proper sections. This procedure is not indispensable, but still it is valuable. Go through the book, and notice the principal divisions among the thoughts. Mark them. Then go through these divisions, find if there are any natural subdivisions, and mark them. In organizing your studies, work from a version of the Bible that is divided according to a logical plan.

Having discovered the divisions of the book, proceed to give each section an appropriate caption. Make this caption as precise a statement of the general contents of the section as possible. Also, make it as brief and as impressionable as you can so that it will fix itself in your mind. Create captions for the subdivisions to connect with the general caption of the division. Do not attempt too complicated a division at first.

The following division of 1 Peter, without many marked subdivisions, will serve as a simple illustration:

- Chapter 1:1–2: Introduction and salutation to the pilgrims and sojourners in Pontus, etc.
- Chapter 1:3–12: The inheritance reserved in heaven and the salvation ready to be revealed for those pilgrims who, in the midst of manifold temptations, are kept by the power of God through faith
- Chapter 1:13–25: The pilgrim's conduct during the days of his pilgrimage
- Chapter 2:1–10: The high calling, position, and destiny of the pilgrim people
- Chapter 2:11–12: The pilgrim's conduct during the days of his pilgrimage
- Chapter 2:13–17: The pilgrim's duty toward the human governments under which he lives
- Chapter 2:18–3:7: The duty of various classes of pilgrims
- Chapter 2:18–25: The duty of servants toward their masters, enforced by an appeal to Christ's conduct under injustice and reviling
- Chapter 3:1–6: The duty of wives toward their husbands
- Chapter 3:7: The duty of husbands toward their wives
- Chapter 3:8–12: The conduct of pilgrims toward one another
- Chapter 3:13–22: The pilgrim suffering for righteousness' sake
- Chapter 4:1–6: The pilgrim's separation from the practices of those among whom he spends the days of his pilgrimage
- Chapter 4:7–11: The pilgrim's sojourning drawing to a close and his conduct during the last days
- Chapter 4:12–19: The pilgrim suffering for and with Christ
- Chapter 5:1–4: The duty and reward of elders
- Chapter 5:5–11: The pilgrim's walk—humble, trustful, watchful, and steadfast—and a doxology
- Chapter 5:12–14: Conclusion and benediction

TAKING BITE-SIZE PIECES

The fifth step is to take each verse in order and study it. In this verse-by-verse study of the book, derive the exact meaning of the verse. How is this to be done? Three steps lead to the meaning of a verse.

First, try to get the exact meaning of the words used. You will find two classes of words: those whose meaning is perfectly apparent and those whose meaning is doubtful. It is quite possible to find the precise meaning of these doubtful words. This is not done, however, by consulting a dictionary. That is an easy, but dangerous, method of finding the scriptural significance of a word. The only safe and sure method is to study the usage of the word in the Bible itself and particularly by the Bible writer whom you are studying.

To study the Bible usage of words, you must have a concordance. In my opinion, the best concordance is *Strong's Exhaustive Concordance of the Bible*. The next best is *Young's Analytical Concordance*. *Cruden's Complete Concordance* will also do if you are on a limited budget. When you are studying a particular word, all the passages in which the word occurs should be found and examined. In this way, the precise meaning of the word will be determined.

Many important Bible doctrines will change the meaning of a word. For example, two schools of theology are divided on the meaning of the word *justify*. The critical question is, does the word *justify* mean "to make righteous" or does it mean "to count or declare righteous"? The correct interpretation of many passages of Scripture hinges on the sense that we give to this word. Look up all the passages in the Bible in which the word is found, and then you will have no doubt as to the Bible usage and meaning of the word. Deuteronomy 25:1; Exodus 23:7; Isaiah 5:23; Luke 16:15; Romans 2:13, 3:23–24, 4:2–8; and Luke 18:14 will serve to illustrate the biblical usage of the word *justify*.

By using *Strong's* or *Young's Concordance*, you will see that the same word may be used in the English version for the translation of several Greek or Hebrew words. Of course, in determining the biblical usage, we should give special attention to those passages in which the English word examined is the translation of the same word in Greek or Hebrew. Either of these concordances will enable you to do this, even though you are not acquainted with Greek or Hebrew. It will be much easier to do, however, with *Strong's Concordance* than with *Young's*.

It is surprising how many knotty problems in the interpretation of Scripture are solved by the simple examination of the biblical usage of words. For example, one of the burning questions of today is the meaning of 1 John 1:7. Does this verse teach that *"the blood of Jesus Christ"* cleanses us from all the guilt of sin or does it teach us that *"the blood of Jesus Christ"* cleanses us from the very presence of sin so that, by the blood of Christ, indwelling sin is itself eradicated?

Many of those who read this question will answer it offhand at once, one way or the other. But the spur-of-the-moment way of answering questions of this kind is a bad way. Take your concordance and look up every passage in the Bible in which the word *cleanse* is used in connection with blood, and the question will be answered conclusively and forever.

Never conclude that you have the right meaning of a verse until you have carefully determined the meaning of all doubtful words in it by an examination of Bible usage. Even when you are fairly sure you know the meaning of the words, it is good not to be too sure until you have looked them up.

LOOK BEHIND AND AHEAD

Now try to ascertain the meaning of a verse by carefully noticing the context (what goes before and what comes after). Many verses, if they stood alone, might be capable of several interpretations. But when the context is considered, all the interpretations except one are seen to be impossible.

For example, in John 14:18, Jesus said, *"I will not leave you comfortless: I will come to you."* What did Jesus mean when He said, *"I will come to you"*? One commentator said, "He refers to His reappearance to His disciples after His resurrection to comfort them." Another said, "He refers to His second coming." Another said, "He refers to His coming through the Holy Spirit's work to manifest Himself to His disciples and make His abode with them."

So what did Jesus mean? When doctors disagree, can an ordinary layman decide? Yes, very often. Certainly in this case. If you will carefully note what Jesus was talking about in the verses immediately preceding (see John 14:15–17) and immediately following (see verses 19–26), you will have no doubt as to what coming Jesus referred to in this passage. You can see this by trying it for yourself.

LOOK AT COMPARISON VERSES

To ascertain the correct and precise meaning of a verse, examine parallel passages—passages that deal with the same subject. For example, study other verses that give another account of the same event or passages that are evidently intended as a commentary on the passage at hand.

Very often, after having carefully studied the context, you may still be in doubt as to which interpretation the writer intended. In this case, there is probably a passage somewhere else in the Bible that will settle this question. In John 14:3, Jesus said, *"I will come again, and receive you unto myself; that where I am, there ye may be also."* A careful consideration of the words used in their relation to one another will help to determine the meaning of this passage.

Still, among commentators, we find four different interpretations. First, the coming referred to here is explained as Christ's coming at death to receive the believer to Himself, as in the case of Stephen. Another commentator interprets this as the coming again at the resurrection. A third sees the coming again through the Holy Spirit. The last defines this passage to be when Christ returns personally and gloriously at the end of the age.

Which of these four interpretations is the correct one? What has already been said about verse 18 might seem to settle the question, but it does not. It is not at all clear that the coming in verse 3 is the same as in verse 18. What is said in connection with the two comings is altogether different. In the one case, it is a coming of Christ to *"receive you unto myself; that where I am, there ye may be also"* (John 14:3). In the other case, it is a coming of Christ to manifest Himself to us and make His abode with us.

Fortunately, there is a passage that settles the question. It is found in 1 Thessalonians 4:16–17. This will be clearly seen if we arrange the two passages in parallel columns.

John 14:3	1 Thessalonians 4:16–17
I will come again,	*The Lord himself shall descend*
	from heaven…
and receive you unto myself;	*we…shall be caught up…*
	to meet the Lord…
that where I am,	*so shall we ever be*
there ye may be also.	*with the Lord.*

The two passages clearly match exactly in the three facts stated. Beyond a doubt, they refer to the same event. Look closely at 1 Thessalonians 4:16–17. There can be no doubt as to what coming of our Lord is referred to here.

These three steps lead us to the meaning of a verse. They require work, but it is work that anyone can do. When the meaning of a verse is settled, you can arrive at conclusions that are correct and fixed. After taking these steps, it is wise to consult commentaries to compare your conclusions to those of others.

> GOD INTENDED TO CONVEY DEFINITE TRUTH IN EACH VERSE OF SCRIPTURE. WITH EVERY VERSE, WE SHOULD ASK WHAT IT WAS *INTENDED* TO TEACH, NOT WHAT IT CAN BE *MADE* TO TEACH; WE SHOULD NOT BE SATISFIED UNTIL WE HAVE SETTLED THIS QUESTION.

Before we proceed to the next step, let me say that God intended to convey definite truth in each verse of Scripture. With every verse, we should ask what it was *intended* to teach, not what it can be *made* to teach; we should not be satisfied until we have settled this question. Of course, I admit a verse may have a primary meaning and then other more remote meanings. For example, a prophecy may have its primary fulfillment in some personage or event near at hand, such as Solomon, with a more remote and complete fulfillment in Christ.

ANALYZING THE VERSE

We are not finished with a verse when we have determined its meaning. The next thing to do is to analyze the verse. The way to do it is this: Look steadfastly at the verse and ask yourself, "What does this verse teach?" Then begin to write down: This verse teaches first ———, second ———, third ———, etc. At first glance, you will see one or two things the verse teaches; but as you look again and again, the teachings will begin to multiply. You will wonder how one verse could teach so much, and you will have an ever growing sense of the divine Author of the Book.

I was once told the story of a professor who had a young man come to him to study ichthyology. The professor gave him a fish to study and told him to come back to get another lesson when he had mastered that fish. In time the young man came back and told the professor what he had observed about the fish. When he had finished, to his surprise, he was given the same fish again and told to study it further. He came back again, having observed new facts about the fish. But again he was given the same fish to study; and so it went on, lesson after lesson, until that student had been taught what his perceptive faculties were for and also how to do thorough work.

We should study the Bible in the same way. We ought to come back to the same verse of the Bible again and again until we have examined, as far as it is possible to us, all that is in the verse. The probability is that when we come back to the same verse several months later, we will find something we did not see before.

An illustration of this method of analysis will be helpful. Look at 1 Peter 1:1–2. (Here is an instance in which the verse division of the King James Version is so clearly illogical that in our analysis we cannot follow it but must take the two verses together. This will often be the case.)

These verses teach:

1. This epistle was written by Peter.
2. The Peter who wrote this epistle was an apostle of Jesus Christ. (*Apostle* is Greek for the word *missionary*.)
3. Peter delighted to think and speak of himself as one sent by Jesus Christ. (Compare 2 Peter 1:1.)
4. The name Jesus Christ is used twice in these two verses. Its significance:
    a. Savior
    b. Anointed One

    c.   Fulfiller of the messianic predictions of the Old Testament. It has special reference to the earthly reign of Christ.

5.   This epistle was written to the elect, especially to the elect who are sojourners of the dispersion in Pontus, that is, Paul's old field of labor.

6.   Believers are:

    a.   Elect or chosen by God.

    b.   Foreknown by God.

    c.   Sanctified by the Spirit.

    d.   Sprinkled by the blood of Jesus Christ.

    e.   Sojourners or pilgrims on earth.

    f.   Subjects of multiplied grace.

    g.   Possessors of multiplied peace.

7.   Election. Who are the elect? Believers. (Compare verse 5.) To what are they elect? Obedience and the sprinkling of the blood of Jesus. According to what are they elect? The foreknowledge of God. (Compare Romans 8:29–30.) In what are they elect? Sanctification of the Spirit. The test of election is obedience. (Compare 2 Peter 1:10.) The work of the three persons of the Trinity in election is this: The Father foreknows, Jesus Christ cleanses sin by His blood, and the Spirit sanctifies.

8.   God is the Father of the elect.

9.   The humanity of Christ is seen in the mention of His blood.

10.   The reality of the body of Jesus Christ is seen in the mention of His blood.

11.   It is by His blood and not by His example that Jesus Christ delivers from sin.

12.   Peter's first and great wish and prayer for those to whom he wrote was that grace and peace might be multiplied.

13.   It is not enough to have grace and peace. One should have multiplied grace and peace.

14. That one already has grace and peace is no reason to cease praying for them but rather an incentive to pray that they may have more grace and peace.

15. Grace precedes peace. Compare all passages where these words are found together.

This is simply an illustration of what is meant by analyzing a verse. The whole book should be gone through in this way.

Three rules must be observed, however, in this analytical work. First, do not put anything into your analysis that is not clearly in the verse. One of the greatest faults in Bible study is reading into passages what God never put into them. Some people have their pet doctrines; they see them everywhere, even where God does not see them. No matter how true, precious, or scriptural a doctrine is, do not put into your analysis what is not in the verse. Considerable experience in this kind of study leads me to emphasize this rule.

Second, find all that is in the verse. This rule can only be carried out relatively. Much will escape you because many of the verses of the Bible are so deep. But do not rest until you have dug and dug and dug, and there seems to be nothing more to find.

Then, state what you do find just as accurately and exactly as possible. Do not be content with putting into your analysis something similar to what is in the verse, but state in your analysis precisely what is in the verse.

CLASSIFYING YOUR RESULTS

Through your verse-by-verse analysis, you have discovered and recorded a great number of facts. The work now is to get these facts organized. To do this, go carefully through your analysis, and note the various subjects in the epistle. Write these subjects down as fast as you find them. Having made a complete list of the subjects dealt with in the book, write these subjects on separate cards or sheets of paper. Then, go through the analysis again and copy each point in the analysis on its appropriate sheet of paper. For example, write every point regarding God the Father on one card or sheet of paper.

This general classification should be followed by a more thorough and minute subdivision. Suppose that you are studying 1 Peter. Having completed your analysis of the epistle and gone over it carefully, you will find that the following subjects are dealt with in this epistle:

+ God
+ Jesus Christ
+ The Holy Spirit
+ The believer
+ Wives and husbands
+ Servants
+ The new birth
+ The Word of God
+ Old Testament Scripture
+ The prophets
+ Prayer
+ Angels
+ The devil
+ Baptism
+ The gospel
+ Salvation
+ The world
+ Gospel preachers and teachers
+ Heaven
+ Humility
+ Love

These will serve as general headings. After the material found in the analysis is arranged under these headings, you will find it easier to divide it into numerous subdivisions. For example, the material under the heading "God" can be divided into these subdivisions:

+ His names: The material under this heading is quite rich.
+ His attributes: This should be subdivided again into His holiness, His power, His foreknowledge, His faithfulness, His long-suffering, His grace, His mercy, His impartiality, and His severity.
+ God's judgments
+ God's will
+ What is acceptable to God?
+ What is due to God?
+ God's dwelling place
+ God's dominion
+ God's work or what God does
+ The things of God: For example, *"the mighty hand of God"* (1 Peter 5:6), *"the house of God"* (1 Peter 4:17), *"the gospel of God"* (verse 17), *"the flock of God"* (1 Peter 5:2), *"the people of God"* (1 Peter 2:10), the

"servants of God" (verse 16), *"the word of God"* (1 Peter 1:23), *"the oracles of God"* (1 Peter 4:11), etc.

To illustrate the classified arrangement of the teaching of a book on one doctrine will probably show you better how to do this work than any abstract statement. It will also illustrate in part how fruitful this method of study is. Look again at 1 Peter and its teachings regarding the believer.

THE BELIEVER'S PRIVILEGES

HIS ELECTION

+ He is foreknown by the Father, 1:2.
+ He is elect or chosen by God, 1:2.
+ He is chosen by God according to His foreknowledge, 1:2.
+ He is chosen to obedience, 1:2.
+ He is chosen for the sprinkling of the blood of Jesus, 1:2.
+ He is chosen in sanctification by the Spirit, 1:2.

HIS CALLING

+ By whom called: God, 1:15; and the God of all grace, 5:10.
+ To what called: the imitation of Christ in the patient taking of suffering for well doing, 2:20–21; to render blessing for reviling, 3:9; out of darkness into God's marvelous light, 2:9; to God's eternal glory, 5:10.
+ In whom called: in Christ, 5:10.
+ The purpose of his calling: that he may show forth the praises of Him who called, 2:9; that he may inherit a blessing, 3:9.

HIS REGENERATION

+ Of God, 1:3.
+ To a living hope, 1:3.
+ To an inheritance incorruptible, undefiled, and that does not fade away, reserved in heaven, 1:4.
+ By the resurrection of Jesus Christ, 1:3.
+ Of incorruptible seed by the Word of God that lives, 1:23.

HIS REDEMPTION

+ Not with corruptible things, such as silver and gold, 1:18.

+ With precious blood, even the blood of Christ, 1:19.

+ From his vain manner of life, handed down from his father, 1:18.

+ His sins have been borne by Christ, in His own body, on the tree, 2:24.

+ His sanctification by the Spirit, 1:2.

+ His cleansing by the blood, 1:2.

+ His security

+ He is guarded by the power of God, 1:5.

+ He is guarded to a salvation ready, or prepared, to be revealed in the last time, 1:5.

+ God cares for him, 5:7.

+ He can cast all his anxiety upon God, 5:7.

+ The God of all grace will perfect, establish, and strengthen him after a brief trial of suffering, 5:10.

+ None can harm him if he is zealous of what is good, 3:13.

+ He will not be put to shame, 2:6.

HIS JOY

+ The character of his joy. Presently, it is an unspeakable joy, 1:8; a joy full of glory, 1:8. This present joy cannot be hindered by being put to grief because of many temptations, 1:6. His future joy is exceeding, 4:13.

+ He rejoices in the salvation prepared to be revealed in the last time, 1:5; in his faith in the unseen Jesus Christ, 1:8; and in fellowship in Christ's sufferings, 4:13.

+ What he will rejoice in: the revelation of Christ's glory, 4:13. Present joy in fellowship with the sufferings of Christ is the condition of exceeding joy at the revelation of Christ's glory, 4:13.

HIS HOPE

+ Its character: a living hope, 1:3; a reasonable hope, 3:15; an inward hope, 3:15.

+ In whom his hope lies: God, 1:21. The foundation of his hope is in the resurrection of Jesus Christ, 1:3–21.

HIS SALVATION

+ A past salvation: He has been redeemed, 1:18–19; and he has been healed, 2:24. By baptism, like Noah by the flood, the believer has passed out of the old life of nature into the new resurrection life of grace, 3:21.

+ A present salvation: He is now receiving the salvation of his soul, 1:9.

+ A growing salvation: through feeding on His Word, 2:2.

+ A future salvation: ready or prepared to be revealed in the last time, 1:5.

THE BELIEVER'S POSSESSIONS

+ God as his Father, 1:17.

+ Christ as his Sin-Bearer, 2:24; example, 2:21; fellow sufferer, 4:13.

+ A living hope, 1:3.

+ An incorruptible, undefiled, and unfading inheritance reserved in heaven, 1:4.

+ Multiplied grace and peace, 1:2.

+ Spiritual milk without guile for his food, 2:2.

+ Gifts for service—each believer has some gift, 4:10.

WHAT BELIEVERS ARE

+ Sojourners or strangers, 1:1.

+ A sojourner on his way to another country, 2:1.

+ A holy priesthood, 2:5.

+ Living stones, 2:5.

+ A spiritual house, 2:5.

+ A chosen generation, 2:9.

+ A royal priesthood, 2:9.

+ A holy nation, 2:9.

+ Partakers of, or partners in, Christ's sufferings, 4:13.

+ Representatives of Christ, 4:16.

+ The house of God, 4:17.

+ Partakers of, or partners in, the glory to be revealed, 5:1.

+ The flock of God, 5:2.

THE BELIEVER'S POSSIBILITIES

+ He may die to sin, 2:24.
+ He may live for righteousness, 2:24.
+ He may follow in Christ's steps, 2:21.
+ He may cease from sin, 4:1.
+ He may cease from living for the lusts of men, 4:2.
+ He may live for the will of God, 4:2.
+ What was for the believer
+ The ministry of the prophets was in his behalf, 1:12.
+ The preciousness of Jesus is for him, 2:7.

UNCLASSIFIED

+ The gospel has been preached to him in the Holy Spirit, 1:12.
+ Grace is to be brought to him at the revelation of Jesus Christ, 1:3. (Compare Ephesians 3:7.)
+ He has tasted that the Lord is gracious, 2:3.

THE BELIEVER'S SUFFERINGS AND TRIALS

+ The fact of the believer's sufferings and trials, 1:6.

THE NATURE OF THE BELIEVER'S SUFFERINGS AND TRIALS

+ He endures grief, suffering wrongfully, 2:19.
+ He suffers for righteousness' sake, 3:14.
+ He suffers for doing good, 3:17; 2:20.
+ He suffers as a Christian, 4:16.
+ He is subjected to many temptations, 1:6.
+ He is put to grief in manifold temptations, 1:6.
+ He is spoken against as an evildoer, 2:12.
+ His good manner of life is reviled, 3:16.
+ He is spoken evil of because of his separated life, 4:4.
+ He is reproached for the name of Christ, 4:14.
+ He is subjected to fiery trials, 4:12.

ENCOURAGEMENT FOR BELIEVERS UNDERGOING FIERY TRIALS AND SUFFERING

+ It is better to suffer for doing good than for doing evil, 3:17.

+ Judgment must begin at the house of God. The present judgment of believers through trial is not comparable to the future end of those who do not obey the gospel, 4:17.

+ Blessed is the believer who suffers for righteousness' sake, 3:14. (Compare Matthew 5:10–12.)

+ Blessed is the believer who is reproached for the name of Christ, 4:14.

+ The Spirit of Glory and of God rests upon the believer who is reproached for the name of Christ, 4:14.

+ The believer's grief is for a little while, 1:6.

+ Suffering for a little while will be followed by God's glory in Christ, which is eternal, 5:10.

+ The suffering endured for a little while is for the testing of faith, 1:7.

+ The fiery trial is for a test, 4:12.

+ The faith thus proved is more precious than gold, 1:7.

+ Faith proven by manifold temptations will be found to praise and honor and glory at the revelation of Jesus Christ, 1:7.

+ His proved faith may result in praise, glory, and honor at the revelation of Jesus Christ, when the believer is for a little while subjected to many temptations, 1:7.

+ It is pleasing to God when a believer takes persecution patiently, when he does well and suffers for it, 2:20.

+ Through suffering in the flesh, we cease from sin, 4:1.

+ Those who speak evil of us will give account to God, 4:5.

+ Sufferings are being shared by fellow believers, 5:9.

+ Christ suffered for us, 2:21.

+ Christ suffered for sins once for all, the righteous for the unrighteous, so that He might bring us to God, being put to death in the flesh, but enlivened by the spirit, 3:18.

+ Christ left the believer an example that he should follow in His steps, 2:21.

+ In our fiery trials, we are made partakers of, or partners in, Christ's sufferings, 4:13.

+ When His glory is revealed, we will be glad with exceeding joy, 4:13.

HOW THE BELIEVER SHOULD MEET HIS TRIAL AND SUFFERINGS

+ The believer should not regard his fiery trial as a strange thing, 4:12.

+ The believer should expect fiery trials, 4:12.

+ When the believer suffers as a Christian, he should not be ashamed, 4:16.

+ When the believer suffers as a Christian, he should glorify God in this matter, 4:16.

+ When the believer suffers, he should not return reviling with reviling, or suffering with threatening, but commit himself to God who judges righteously, 2:23.

+ When the believer suffers, he should commit the keeping of his soul to God, as to a faithful Creator, 4:19.

THE BELIEVER'S DANGERS

+ The believer may fall into fleshly lusts that war against the soul, 2:11.

+ The believer may sin, 2:20.

+ The believer may fall into sins of the gravest character, 4:15. (Note in this verse the awful possibilities that lie dormant in the heart of a sincere, professed believer.)

+ The believer's prayers may be hindered, 3:7.

+ The believer is in danger that his high calling and destiny may tempt him to despise human laws and authority, 2:13.

+ The believer is in danger that his high calling may lead him to lose sight of his lowly obligations to human masters, 2:18.

+ Young believers are in danger of disregarding the will and authority of older believers, 5:5.

THE BELIEVER'S RESPONSIBILITY

+ Each believer has an individual responsibility, 4:10.

+ Each believer's responsibility is for the gift he has received, 4:10.

THE BELIEVER'S DUTIES

WHAT THE BELIEVER SHOULD BE

+ Be holy in all manner of living because God is holy, 1:15; and because it is written, *"Be ye holy, for I am holy"* (verse 16).

+ Be like Him who called him, 1:15–16.

+ Be sober, or of a calm, collected, thoughtful spirit, 1:13; 4:7; 5:8.

+ Be serious in prayer, 4:7.

+ Be of a sound mind; the end of all things is approaching, 4:7.

+ Be watchful, 5:8.

+ Be steadfast in the faith, 5:9.

+ Be subject to every ordinance of man for the Lord's sake, 2:13; to the king as supreme, 2:13; to government officials who are sent by the king to punish evildoers and to praise those who do well, 2:14; because this is God's will, 2:15.

+ Be of one mind, 3:8.

+ Be compassionate, 3:8.

+ Be tenderhearted, 3:8.

+ Be courteous, 3:8.

+ Be ready always to give an answer to everyone who asks a reason for the hope that is in him, with meekness and fear, 3:15; in order to put to shame those who revile his good conduct in Christ, 3:16.

+ Be not troubled, 3:14.

WHAT THE BELIEVER SHOULD NOT DO

+ The believer should not conform himself to the lusts of the old life of ignorance, 1:14.

+ The believer should not return evil for evil, 3:9.

+ The believer should not return reviling for reviling, 3:9.

+ The believer should not be afraid of the world's threats, 3:14.

+ The believer should not live his remaining time in the flesh for the lusts of men, 4:2.

WHAT THE BELIEVER SHOULD DO

+ Live as a child of obedience, 1:14.

+ Pass the time of his sojourning here in fear of the Lord, 1:17.

+ Abstain from fleshly lusts that war against the soul, 2:11.

+ Observe God's will as the absolute law of life, 2:15.

+ Let his conscience be governed by the thought of God and not by the conduct of men, 2:19.

+ Sanctify Christ in his heart as Lord, 3:15. (Compare Isaiah 8:13.)

+ Live his remaining time in the flesh to the will of God, 4:2.

+ Put away all malice, 2:1; all deceit, 2:1; hypocrisy, 2:1; envy, 2:1; all evil speaking, 2:1.

+ Come to the Lord as to a living stone, 2:4.

+ Proclaim the praises of Him who called him out of darkness into His marvelous light, 2:9.

+ Arm himself with the mind of Christ, that is, to suffer in the flesh, 4:1.

+ Cast all his care upon God because He cares for him, 5:7.

+ Stand fast in the true grace of God, 5:12.

+ Resist the devil, 5:9.

+ Humble himself under the mighty hand of God: because God resists the proud and gives grace to the humble, 5:5; so that God may exalt him in due time, 5:6.

+ Glorify God when he suffers as a Christian, 4:16.

+ See to it that he does not suffer as a thief, an evildoer, or a meddler in other people's matters, 4:15.

+ Rejoice in fiery trials, 4:13.

+ Toward various persons: toward God—fear, 2:17; toward the king—honor, 2:17; toward masters—be in subjection with all fear (not only to the good and gentle, but also to the harsh), 2:18; toward the brethren—love, 1:22; 2:17; 4:8; toward his revilers—blessing for reviling, 3:9; toward the Gentiles—honorable conduct, 2:12 (that God may be glorified); toward foolish men—by doing good, put to silence their ignorance, 2:15; and toward all people—honor, 2:17.

+ Desire the pure milk of the Word, 2:2.

+ Gird up the loins of his mind, 1:13.

+ Grow, 2:2.

+ Hope fully on the grace that is to be brought to him at the revelation of Jesus Christ, 1:13.

THE BELIEVER'S CHARACTERISTICS

+ His faith and hope are in God, 1:21.

+ He believes in God through Jesus Christ, 1:21.

+ He calls on God as Father, 1:17.

+ He believes in Christ, though he has never seen Him, 1:8.

+ He loves Christ, though he has never seen Him, 1:8.

+ He has returned to the Shepherd and Overseer of his soul, 2:25.

+ He has purified his soul in obedience to the truth, 1:22.

+ He has sincere love for the brethren, 1:22.

+ He has good conduct, 3:16.

+ He does not run with the Gentiles among whom he lives, to the same excess of riot, but lives a separated life, 4:4.

+ He refrains his tongue from evil, 3:10, and refrains his lips so that they speak no deceit, 3:10.

+ He turns away from evil, 3:11.

+ He does good, 3:11.

+ He seeks peace, 3:11.

+ He pursues peace, 3:11.

THE BELIEVER'S WARFARE

+ The believer has a warfare before him, 4:1.

+ The mind of Christ is the proper armament for this warfare, 4:1.

+ The warfare is with the devil, 5:8–9.

+ Victory is possible for the believer, 5:9.

+ Victory is won through steadfastness in the faith, 5:9.

HOW TO RETAIN YOUR STUDIES

At first thought, it may seem that when we had completed our classification of results, our work was finished, but this is not so. These results are for use: first, for personal enjoyment and appropriation, and afterward to give to others. To obtain results, you must meditate on them.

We are no more through with a book when we have carefully and fully classified its contents than we are through with a meal when we have arranged it in an orderly way on the table. It is there to eat, digest, and assimilate.

One of the greatest failures in Bible study today is at this point. There is observation, analysis, classification, but no meditation. Perhaps nothing is as important in Bible study as meditation. (See Joshua 1:8; Psalm 1:2–3.)

> ONE OF THE GREATEST FAILURES IN BIBLE STUDY TODAY IS WHEN THERE IS OBSERVATION, ANALYSIS, CLASSIFICATION, BUT NO MEDITATION. PERHAPS NOTHING IS AS IMPORTANT IN BIBLE STUDY AS MEDITATION.

Take your classified teachings and go slowly over them. Ponder them, point by point, until these wonderful truths live before you, sink into your soul, and become part of your life. Do this again and again. Nothing will go further than meditation to make you become a great, fresh, and original thinker and speaker. Very few people in this world are great thinkers.

The method of study outlined in this chapter can be shortened to suit the time and vocation of the student. For example, you can omit the verse-by-verse study and proceed at once to go through the book as a whole and note its teachings on different doctrines. This will greatly shorten and lighten the work. It will also greatly detract from the richness of the results, however, and will not be as thorough, accurate, or as scholarly. But anyone can be, if he will, a scholar, at least in the most important work: that of biblical study.

CHAPTER 3

TOPICAL STUDY

A second method of Bible study, perhaps the most fascinating, is the topical method. This consists in searching through the Bible to find out what its teaching is on various topics. The only way to master any subject is to go through the Bible and find what it has to teach on that topic. Almost any great subject will take a remarkable hold on the heart of a Christian, if he will take time to go through the Bible from Genesis to Revelation and note what it has to say on that topic. He will have a fuller, more correct understanding of that specific area than he ever had before.

D. L. Moody once said that he studied the word *grace* in this way. Day after day, he went through the Bible, studying what it had to say about *grace*. As the Bible doctrine unfolded before his mind, his heart began to burn, until at last, full of the subject and on fire with the subject, he ran onto the street. Taking hold of the first man he met, he said, "Do you know grace?"

"Grace who?" was the reply.

"The grace of God that brings salvation."

Then he poured out his soul on that subject.

If any child of God will study grace, love, faith, prayer, or any other great Bible doctrine in this way, his soul, too, will become filled with it. Jesus evidently studied the Old Testament Scriptures in this way. *"Beginning at Moses and all the prophets, he expounded unto them in all the scriptures the things concerning himself"* (Luke 24:27). This method of study made the hearts of the two who walked with Him burn within them. (See Luke 24:32.) Paul seemed to have followed his Master in this method of study and teaching. (See Acts 17:2–3.)

WATCH OUT FOR IMBALANCE

This method of topical study has its dangers, however. Many are drawn by the fascination of this method to give up all other methods of study, and this is a great misfortune. A well-rounded, thorough knowledge of the Bible is not possible by one method of study alone.

But the greatest danger lies in this: everyone is almost certain to have some topics in which he is especially interested. If he studies his Bible topically, unless he is warned, he is more than likely to focus on certain topics repeatedly. Thus, he will be very strong in certain areas of truth, but other topics of equal importance may be neglected, and he may become one-sided.

We never know one truth correctly until we know it in its proper relationship to other truths. I know of people, for example, who are interested in the great doctrine of the Lord's second coming. Therefore, almost all their Bible studies are on that line. Now this is a precious doctrine, but there are other doctrines in the Bible that a person needs to know; it is folly to study this doctrine alone.

I know others whose whole interest and study seem to focus on the subject of divine healing. One man confided to a friend that he had devoted years to the study of the number seven in the Bible. This is doubtless an extreme case, but it illustrates the danger in topical study. It is certain that we will never master the whole range of Bible truth if we pursue the topical method alone. A few rules concerning topical study will probably be helpful to you.

Don't follow your fancy in the choice of topics. Don't take up any topic that happens to suggest itself. Make a list of all the subjects you can think of that are touched on in the Bible. Make it as comprehensive and complete as possible. Then study these topics one by one in logical order. The following list of subjects is given as a suggestion. Each person can add to the list for himself and separate the general subjects into proper subdivisions.

LIST OF TOPICS

GOD

+ God as a Spirit

+ The unity of God

- The eternity of God
- The omnipresence of God
- The personality of God
- The omnipotence of God
- The omniscience of God
- The holiness of God

- The love of God
- The righteousness of God
- The mercy or lovingkindness of God
- The faithfulness of God
- The grace of God

JESUS CHRIST

- The divinity of Christ
- The subordination of Christ to God
- The human nature of Jesus Christ
- The character of Jesus Christ

  » His holiness

  » His love for God

  » His love for man

  » His love for souls

  » His compassion

  » His prayer life

  » His meekness and humility

- The death of Jesus Christ

  » The purpose of Christ's death

  » Why did Christ die?

  » For whom did Christ die?

  » The results of Christ's death

- The resurrection of Jesus Christ

  » The fact of the resurrection

  » The results of the resurrection

  » The importance of the resurrection

  » The manner of the resurrection

- The ascension and exaltation of Christ
- The return or coming again of Christ

- » The fact of His coming again
- » The manner of His coming again
- » The purpose of His coming again
- » The result of His coming again
- » The time of His coming again
- The reign of Jesus Christ

THE HOLY SPIRIT

- The personality of the Holy Spirit
- The deity of the Holy Spirit
- The distinction of the Holy Spirit
- The subordination of the Holy Spirit
- The names of the Holy Spirit
- The work of the Holy Spirit

  - » In the universe
  - » In man in general
  - » In the believer
  - » In the prophet and apostle
  - » In Jesus Christ

MAN

- His original condition
- His fall
- His standing before God
- The future destiny of unbelievers
- Justification
- The new birth
- Adoption
- The believer's assurance of salvation
- The flesh
- Sanctification
- Cleansing
- Consecration
- Faith
- Repentance
- Prayer
- Thanksgiving
- Praise
- Worship
- Love for God
- Love for Jesus Christ
- Love for man
- The future destiny of believers

ANGELS

- ✦ Their nature and position
- ✦ Their number
- ✦ Their abode
- ✦ Their character
- ✦ Their work
- ✦ Their destiny

SATAN OR THE DEVIL

- ✦ His existence
- ✦ His nature and position
- ✦ His abode
- ✦ His work
- ✦ Our duty regarding him
- ✦ His destiny

DEMONS

- ✦ Their existence
- ✦ Their nature
- ✦ Their work
- ✦ Their destiny

For the student who has the perseverance to carry it through, it might be recommended to begin with the first topic on a list like this and go right through to the end, searching for everything the Bible has to say on these topics. I have done this and, thereby, gained a fuller knowledge of truth than I ever obtained by extended studies in systematic theology.

Many, however, will stagger at the seeming immensity of the undertaking. To such, it is recommended to begin by selecting those topics that seem more important, but sooner or later, settle down to a thorough study of what the Bible has to teach about God and man.

BE THOROUGH

Whenever you are studying any topic, do not be content with examining some of the passages in the Bible that pertain to the subject. As far as possible, find every passage in the Bible that relates to this subject. As long as there is a single passage in the Bible on any subject that you have not considered, you have not yet acquired a thorough knowledge of that subject.

How can you find all the passages in the Bible that relate to any subject? First, by the use of a concordance. Look up every passage that has the word in it. Then look up every passage that has synonyms of that word in it. If, for example, you are studying the subject of prayer, look up every passage that has the word *pray* and its derivatives in it and also every passage that has such words as *cry, call, ask, supplication, intercession,* and so forth.

You may also use a topical Bible, such as *Nave's Topical Bible: A Digest of the Holy Scriptures.* This book arranges the passages of Scripture by the subjects discussed.

Finally, passages not discovered by use of either a concordance or topical guide will come to light as you study by books or as you read the Bible through. In this way, the number of topics we deal with will be ever broadening.

GETTING THE EXACT MEANING

Study each passage in its context and find its meaning in the way suggested in the chapter on chapter 2, "Individual Book Study."

Topical study is frequently carried on in a very careless fashion. Passages taken out of context are strung or huddled together because of some superficial connection with one another without regard to their real sense and teaching.

> TOPICAL STUDY IS FREQUENTLY CARRIED ON IN A VERY CARELESS FASHION. PASSAGES TAKEN OUT OF CONTEXT ARE STRUNG OR HUDDLED TOGETHER BECAUSE OF SOME SUPERFICIAL CONNECTION WITH ONE ANOTHER WITHOUT REGARD TO THEIR REAL SENSE AND TEACHING.

This has brought the whole method of topical study into disrepute. But it is possible to be as exact and scholarly in topical study as in any other method when the results are instructive and gratifying and not misleading. But the results are sure to be misleading and unsatisfactory if the work is done in a careless, inexact way.

HOW TO ARRANGE YOUR NOTES

In studying any large subject, you will obtain a large amount of written material. Having obtained it, it must now be organized into a logical study form. As you look it over carefully, you will soon see the facts that belong together. Arrange them together in a logical order. For instance, perhaps you have accumulated much material on the deity of Jesus Christ. An example of topical study may be arranged as follows:

JESUS CHRIST: HIS DEITY

DIVINE NAMES

"*The Son of God*" (Luke 22:70). This name is given to Christ forty times. Additionally, the synonymous expression *His Son* or *My Son* frequently occur. This name of Christ is a distinctly divine name that indicates Jesus' relationship with God, His Father. (See John 5:18.)

"*The only begotten Son*" (John 1:18). This name occurs five times. It is not true when people say that Jesus Christ is the Son of God only in the same sense that all men are sons of God. (Compare Mark 12:6.) Here Jesus Himself, having spoken of all the prophets as servants of God, speaks of Himself as "*one son, his well-beloved.*"

"*The first and the last*" (Revelation 1:17). (Compare Isaiah 41:4; 44:6.) In these latter passages, it is "*the LORD of hosts*" who is "*the first, and…the last*" (Isaiah 44:6).

The "*Alpha and Omega*" or "*the beginning and the end*" (Revelation 22:13). In Revelation 1:8, it is the Lord who is "*Alpha and Omega.*"

"*The Holy One*" (Acts 3:14). In Hosea 11:9 and many other passages, it is God who is "the Holy One."

"*The Lord.*" (See, for example, Malachi 3:1; Luke 2:11; Acts 9:17; John 20:28; Hebrews 1:10.) This name or title is used of Jesus several hundred times. He is spoken of as the Lord just as God is. (Compare Acts 4:26 with 4:33. Note also Matthew 22:43–45, Philippians 2:11, and Ephesians 4:5.) If anyone doubts the attitude of the apostles of Jesus toward Him as divine, they would do well to read one after another the passages that speak of Him as Lord.

"*Lord of all*" (Acts 10:36).

"*The Lord of glory*" (1 Corinthians 2:8). In Psalm 24:10, it is "*the LORD of hosts*" who is "*the King of glory.*"

"*Wonderful, Counsellor, The mighty God, The everlasting Father, The Prince of Peace*" (Isaiah 9:6).

"*God*" (Hebrews 1:8). In John 20:28, Thomas calls Jesus "*my God*" and is gently rebuked for not believing it before. (See verse 29.)

"*God with us*" (Matthew 1:23).

"*The great God*" (Titus 2:13).

"*God blessed for ever*" (Romans 9:5).

Conclusion: Sixteen names clearly implying deity are used of Christ in the Bible, some of them over and over again, the total number of passages reaching into the hundreds.

DIVINE ATTRIBUTES

OMNIPOTENCE

Jesus has power over disease. It is subject to His word. (See Luke 4:39.)

The Son of God has power over death. It is subject to His word. (See Luke 7:14–15; 8:54–55; John 5:25.)

Jesus has power over the winds and sea. They are subject to His word. (See Matthew 8:26–27.)

Jesus the Christ, the Son of God, has power over demons. They are subject to His word. (See Matthew 8:16; Luke 4:35–36, 41.)

Christ is far above *all* principality, power, might, dominion, and every name that is named, not only in this world but also in the one to come. All things are in subjection under His feet. All the hierarchies of the angelic world are under Him. (See Ephesians 1:20–23.)

The Son of God upholds *all* things by the word of His power. (Hebrews 1:3.)

Conclusion: Jesus Christ, the Son of God, is omnipotent.

OMNISCIENCE

Jesus knows men's lives, even their secret histories. (See John 4:16–19.)

Jesus knows the secret thoughts of men. He knew all men. He knew what was in man. (See Mark 2:8; Luke 5:22; John 2:24–25.)

Jesus knew from the beginning that Judas would betray Him. Not only men's present thoughts, but also their future choices were known to Him. (See John 6:64.)

Jesus knew what men were doing at a distance. (See John 1:48.)

Jesus knew the future regarding not only God's acts but also the minute, specific acts of men. (See Luke 5:4–6; Luke 22:10–12; John 13:1.)

Jesus knew all things. In Him are hidden all the treasures of wisdom and knowledge. (See John 16:30; 21:17; Colossians 2:3.)

Conclusion: Jesus Christ is omniscient.

OMNIPRESENCE

Jesus Christ is present in every place where two or three are gathered together in His name. (See Matthew 18:20.)

Jesus Christ is present with everyone who goes forth into any part of the world to make disciples. (See Matthew 28:19–20.)

Jesus Christ is in each believer. (See John 14:20; 2 Corinthians 13:5.)

Jesus Christ fills all in all. (See Ephesians 1:23.)

Conclusion: Jesus Christ is omnipresent.

ETERNAL

Jesus is eternal. (See Isaiah 9:7; Micah 5:2; John 1:1; John 17:5; Colossians 1:17; Hebrews 13:8.)

Conclusion: The Son of God was from all eternity.

IMMUTABLE

Jesus Christ is unchangeable. He not only always is but always is *the same*. (See Hebrews 1:12; 13:8.)

Conclusion: Five or more distinctively divine attributes are ascribed to Jesus Christ, and all the fullness of the Godhead is said to dwell in Him. (See Colossians 2:9.)

DIVINE OFFICES

The Son of God, the eternal Word, the Lord, is Creator of all created things. (See John 1:3; Colossians 1:16; and Hebrews 1:10.)

The Son of God is the preserver of all things. (See Hebrews 1:3.)

Jesus Christ had power on earth to forgive sins. (See Mark 2:5–10; Luke 7:48–50.)

Jesus Christ raised the dead. (See John 6:39–44; 5:28–29.) Question: Did not Elijah and Elisha raise the dead? No, God raised the dead in answer to their prayers, but Jesus Christ will raise the dead by His own word. During the days of His humiliation, it was by prayer that Christ raised the dead.

Jesus Christ will fashion anew the body of our humiliation into the likeness of His own glorious body. (See Philippians 3:21.)

Christ Jesus will judge the living and the dead. (See 2 Timothy 4:1.)

Jesus Christ is the giver of eternal life. (See John 10:28; 17:2.)

Conclusion: Seven distinctively divine offices belong to Jesus Christ.

OLD TESTAMENT STATEMENTS MADE DISTINCTLY ABOUT JEHOVAH GOD REFER TO JESUS CHRIST IN THE NEW TESTAMENT

+ Numbers 21:6–7. Compare 1 Corinthians 10:9.
+ Psalm 23:1; Isaiah 40:10–11. Compare John 10:11.
+ Psalm 102:24–27. Compare Hebrews 1:10–12.
+ Isaiah 3:10; 6:1. Compare John 12:37–4 1.
+ Isaiah 8:12–13. Compare I Peter 3:14–15.
+ Isaiah 8:13–14. Compare 1 Peter 2:7–8.
+ Isaiah 40:3–4. Compare Matthew 3:3; Luke 1:68–69, 76.
+ Isaiah 60:19; Zechariah 2:5. Compare Luke 2:32.
+ Jeremiah 11:20; 17:10. Compare Revelation 2:23.
+ Ezekiel 34:11–12, 16. Compare Luke 19:10.

"Lord" in the Old Testament always refers to God except when the context clearly indicates otherwise. "Lord" in the New Testament always refers to Jesus Christ except where the context clearly indicates otherwise.

Conclusion: Many statements in the Old Testament made distinctly of Jehovah God are taken in the New Testament to refer to Jesus Christ. In New Testament thought and doctrine, Jesus Christ occupies the place that Jehovah occupies in Old Testament thought and doctrine.

NAMES OF GOD THE FATHER AND JESUS CHRIST THE SON COUPLED TOGETHER

+ 2 Corinthians 13:14
+ Matthew 28:19
+ 1 Thessalonians 3:11
+ 1 Corinthians 12:4–6
+ Titus 3:4–5. Compare Titus 2:13.
+ Romans 1:7 (See all the Pauline Epistles.)
+ James 1:1
+ John 14:23, "We," that is, God and Jesus Christ
+ 2 Peter 1:1
+ Colossians 2:2
+ John 17:3
+ John 14:1. Compare Jeremiah 17:5–7.
+ Revelation 7:10
+ Revelation 5:13. Compare John 5:23.

Conclusion: The name of Jesus Christ is coupled with that of God the Father in numerous passages in a way in which it would be impossible to couple the name of any finite being with that of the deity.

DIVINE WORSHIP IS TO BE GIVEN TO JESUS CHRIST

Jesus Christ accepted without hesitation a worship that good men and angels declined with fear (horror). (See Matthew 4:9–10; 14:33; 28:8–9; Luke 24:52. Compare Acts 10:25–26 and Revelation 22:8–9.)

Prayer is to be made to Christ. (See Acts 7:59; 1 Corinthians 1:2; 2 Corinthians 12:8–9.)

It is God the Father's will that all men pay the same divine honor to the Son as to Himself. (See Psalm 45:11; John 5:23. Compare Revelation 5:8–9, 12–13.)

The Son of God, Jesus, is to be worshipped as God by angels and men.

Conclusion: Jesus Christ is a person to be worshipped by angels and men even as God the Father is worshipped.

Conclusion: By the use of numerous divine names, by attributing all the distinctively divine attributes, by the affirmation of several divine offices, by referring statements that in the Old Testament distinctly name Jehovah God as their subject to Jesus Christ in the New Testament, by coupling the name of Jesus Christ with that of God the Father in a way in which it would be impossible to couple that of any finite being with that of the deity, and by the clear teaching that Jesus Christ should be worshipped even as God the Father is worshipped—in all these unmistakable ways—God's Word distinctly proclaims that Jesus Christ is a divine being and is indeed God.

One suggestion remains in regard to topical study: Choose further subjects for topical study from your own book studies.

CHAPTER 4

BIOGRAPHICAL STUDY

A third method of study is the biographical study, which consists in studying the life, work, and character of various people mentioned in Scripture. It is a special form of topical study that can be particularly useful to ministers as they prepare their sermons. The following suggestions will help those who are not already experienced in this line of work.

Using *Strong's Concordance*, collect all the passages in the Bible that mention the person to be studied.

Analyze the character of the person. This will require a repeated reading of the passages in which he is mentioned. This should be done with pen in hand so that any characteristic may be noted at once.

Note the elements of power and success.

Note the elements of weakness and failure.

Note the difficulties overcome.

Note the helps to success.

Note the privileges abused.

Note the opportunities neglected.

Note the opportunities improved.

Note the mistakes made.

Note the perils avoided.

Make a sketch of the life in hand. Make it as vivid, living, and realistic as possible. Try to reproduce the subject as a real, living person. Note the place and surroundings of the different events, for example, Paul in Athens, Corinth, or Philippi. Note the time relationships of different events. Very few people take notice of the rapid passage of time when they read the Acts of the Apostles. They regard events that are separated by years as following one another in close sequence. In this connection, note the age or approximate age of the subject at the time of the events recorded.

Summarize the lessons we should learn from the story of this person's life.

Note the person's relationship to Jesus as a type of Christ (Joseph, David, Solomon, and others), a forerunner of Christ, a believer in Christ, an enemy of Christ, a servant of Christ, a brother of Christ (James and Jude), a friend, and so forth.

Begin with some person who does not occupy too much space in the Bible, such as Enoch or Stephen. Of course, many of the points mentioned above cannot be applied to some characters.

CHAPTER 5

STUDY OF TYPES

A fourth method is the study of types. Both an interesting and instructive method, it shows us precious truths buried away in seemingly dry and meaningless portions of the Bible. This method of study is, however, greatly abused and overdone by some people. But that is no reason why we should neglect it altogether, especially when we remember that not only Paul but also Jesus was fond of this method of study. The following principles may guide us in this study.

Be sure you have a biblical authority for your supposed type. If one gives free rein to his suppositions, he can imagine types everywhere, even in places that neither the human nor the divine Author of the book intended. Never say something is a type unless you can point to some clear passage of Scripture where types are definitely taught.

Begin with simple and evident types, such as the Passover (compare Exodus 12 with 1 Corinthians 5:7), the high priest, or the tabernacle.

Guard against an over-strained imagination. Anyone blessed with imagination and quickness of typical discernment will find his imagination running away unless he holds it in check.

In studying any passage where types may be suggested, look up all scriptural references in a reliable concordance. Study carefully the meaning of the names of people and places mentioned. Bible names often have a deep and far-reaching suggestiveness. For example, Hebron, which means "joining together," "union," or "fellowship," is deeply significant when taken in connection with its history, as are all the names of the cities of refuge. Was it accidental that Bethlehem, the name of the place where the Bread of Life was born, means "house of bread"?

CHAPTER 6

STUDY OF BIBLICAL AND CHRONOLOGICAL ORDER

A fifth method of Bible study is the old-fashioned method of biblical order, beginning at Genesis and going right on through to Revelation. This method has some advantages that no other methods of study possess. Start at the beginning of this library of sixty-six books and read right through. It is important to master the Bible as a whole in order to understand the separate books in it.

There are advantages to studying the Bible in scriptural order. First, it is the only method by which you will get an idea of the Book as a whole. The more you know of the Bible as a whole, the better prepared you will be to understand any individual portion of it. Second, it is the only method by which you are likely to cover the whole Book and so take in the entire scope of God's revelation. This is a time-consuming but rewarding way to study the Bible.

Every part of God's Word is precious. Hidden away in the most unexpected places, such as 1 Chronicles 4:10, you will find priceless gems. It is also the best method to enable one to get hold of the unity of the Bible and its organic character.

The Bible is a many-sided book. It clearly teaches the deity of Christ and insists on His real humanity. It exalts faith and demands works. It urges to victory through conflict and asserts most vigorously that victory is won by faith.

If you become too one-sided with any line of truth, the daily, orderly study of the Bible will soon bring you to some contrasted line of truth and back to proper balance. Some people have become mentally distracted through too much occupation with a single line of truth. Thoughtful study of the whole Bible is a great corrective to this tendency.

THE BIBLE CLEARLY TEACHES THE DEITY OF CHRIST AND INSISTS ON HIS REAL HUMANITY. IT EXALTS FAITH AND DEMANDS WORKS. IT URGES TO VICTORY THROUGH CONFLICT AND ASSERTS MOST VIGOROUSLY THAT VICTORY IS WON BY FAITH.

It would be good to have three methods of study in progress at the same time: first, the study of a particular book; second, the study of topics (perhaps topics suggested by the book being studied); third, the study of the Bible in a progressive and organized fashion. Every other method of study should be supplemented by studying the Bible in biblical order. Some years ago, I determined to read a different version of the Bible and the New Testament in Greek through every year. It proved exceedingly profitable in my own studies.

STUDYING BY CHRONOLOGICAL ORDER

Another method of study closely related to the above method has advantages of its own. It is studying the various portions of the Bible in their chronological order. In this way, the Psalms are read in their historical settings, as are prophecies, epistles, and so on.

CHAPTER 7

STUDY FOR PRACTICAL USE IN DEALING WITH PEOPLE

The last method of Bible study is for use in dealing with people. To study the Bible in this way, make as complete a classification as possible of all the different personalities that you find in the world today. Write the names of these various types at the head of separate sheets of paper or cards. Then begin reading the Bible through slowly. When you come to a passage that seems likely to prove useful in dealing with a certain personality type, write it down on the appropriate sheet. Go through the entire Bible in this way. Use special Bible markers in different colored inks or use different letters or symbols to represent the personalities. The best book is the one you organize yourself. My book entitled *How to Bring Men to Christ* may give you some suggestions on how to begin.

The following list of types of people are suggestions to which you can add.

+ The careless and indifferent
+ Those who wish to be saved but do not know how
+ Those who know how to be saved but have difficulties. They may be further categorized with statements, such as:

  » I am too great a sinner.
  » My heart is too hard.
  » I must become better before I become a Christian.
  » I am afraid I can't hold out.
  » I am too weak.
  » I have tried before and failed.
  » I cannot give up my evil ways.
  » I will be persecuted if I become a Christian.
  » It will hurt my business.

» There is too much to give up.

» The Christian life is too hard.

» I am afraid of ridicule.

» I will lose my friends.

» I have no feeling.

» I have been seeking Christ but cannot find Him.

» God won't receive me.

» I have committed the unpardonable sin.

» It is too late.

» Christians are so inconsistent.

» God seems to me unjust and cruel.

» There are so many things in the Bible that I can't under-stand.

» There is someone I can't forgive.

Perhaps you will meet people who are cherishing false hopes. Their hope lies in being saved by a righteous life or by being saved by trying to be a good Christian. They may feel saved because of a profession of religion or church membership.

Others on your list may include those who wish to put off the decision to be saved, such as Jews, spiritualists, or Christian Scientists. You may also add to your list: the sorrowing, the persecuted, the discouraged, the despondent, or the worldly Christian.

The results of this work will be of incalculable value. You will get a new view of how perfectly the Bible is adapted to everyone's need. Familiar passages of the Bible will take on new meaning as you see their relationship to people's needs. In seeking food for others, you will get a vast amount of material to use in sermons, in teaching, and in personal work. You will acquire a rare working knowledge of the Bible.

CHAPTER 8

FINAL SUGGESTIONS

Some suggestions remain to be given before I close this book. First of all, study the Bible regularly. Regularity counts more in Bible study than most people can imagine. The spasmodic student who sometimes gives a great deal of time to the study of the Word and at other times neglects it for days does not achieve the same results as the one who plods on faithfully day by day. The Bereans were wise *"with all readiness of mind"* in that they *"searched the scriptures daily"* (Acts 17:11).

A well-known speaker among Christian college students once remarked that he had been at many conventions and had received great blessings from them, but the greatest blessing he had ever received was from a convention where only three people gathered together with him. These four had covenanted together to spend a certain portion of every day in Bible study. Since that day, much of his time had been spent in cars, in hotels, and at conventions, but he had kept that covenant. The greatest blessing that had come to him in his Christian life had come through this daily study of the Word.

Anyone who has tried it realizes how much can be accomplished by setting apart a fixed portion of each day for Bible study. You may study as little as fifteen or thirty minutes, but it is better to have an hour kept sacredly for that purpose under all circumstances.

> NOTHING IS MORE IMPORTANT THAN DAILY BIBLE STUDY, AND LESS IMPORTANT THINGS MUST NOT TAKE ITS PLACE. WHAT REGULARITY IN EATING IS TO PHYSICAL LIFE, REGULARITY IN BIBLE STUDY IS TO SPIRITUAL LIFE.

Many will say, "I cannot spare the time." It will not do to study the Bible only when you feel like it or when you have leisure. You must have fixed habits if you are to study the Bible profitably. Nothing is more important than daily Bible study, and less important things must not take its place. What regularity in eating is to physical life, regularity in Bible study is to spiritual life. Decide upon some time, even if it is no more than fifteen minutes to start with, and hold to it until you are ready to set a longer period.

SELECT THE CORRECT TIME

Don't put off your Bible study until nearly bedtime when your mind is drowsy. It is good to meditate on God's Word as you retire, but this is not the time for study. Bible study demands a clear mind. Don't take the time immediately after a heavy meal when you are mentally and physically sluggish. It is almost the unanimous opinion of those who have given this subject careful attention that the early hours of the day are the best for Bible study, if they can be free from interruption. Wherever possible, lock yourself in and lock the world out to concentrate fully on the Word of God.

LOOK FOR JESUS

We read of Jesus that *"beginning at Moses and all the prophets, he expounded unto them in all the scriptures the things concerning himself"* (Luke 24:27). Jesus Christ is the subject of the whole Bible, and He pervades the entire Book. Some of the seemingly driest portions become infused with a new life when we learn to see Christ in them. I remember in my early reading what a dull book Leviticus seemed, but it all became different when I learned to see Jesus in the various offerings and sacrifices, in the high priest and his garments, in the tabernacle and its furniture, and indeed everywhere. Look for Christ in every verse you study, and even the genealogies and the names of towns will begin to have beauty and power.

MEMORIZE SCRIPTURE

The psalmist said, *"Thy word have I hid in mine heart, that I might not sin against thee"* (Psalm 119:11). There is nothing better to keep one from sinning than this. By the Word of God hidden in His heart, Jesus overcame the Tempter. (See Matthew 4:4, 7, 10.)

But the Word of God hidden in the heart is good for other purposes than victory over sin. It is good to meet and expose error. It is good to enable one *"to speak a word in season to him that is weary"* (Isaiah 50:4). It is good for manifold uses, even *"that the man of God may be perfect, thoroughly furnished unto all good works"* (2 Timothy 3:17).

Memorize Scripture by chapter and verse. It is just as easy as memorizing a few words, and it is immeasurably more useful for practical purposes. Memorize Scripture in systematic form. Do not have a chaotic heap of texts in your mind, but pigeonhole the Scripture you store in memory under appropriate titles. Then you can bring it out when you need it, without racking your brain. Many can stand up without a moment's warning and speak coherently and convincingly on any vital theme because they have a vast fund of wisdom in Scripture texts stored away in their mind in systematic form.

USE SPARE MOMENTS

Most of us waste too much time. Time spent traveling, waiting for appointments, or waiting for meals can be used in Bible study if you will carry a pocket Bible or pocket Testament. You can also use the time to meditate on texts already stored away in memory.

Henry Ward Beecher read one of the larger histories of England through while waiting day after day for his meals to be brought to the table. How many books of the Bible could be studied in the same way? A friend once told me about a man who had, in some respect, the most extraordinary knowledge of the Bible of any man he knew. This man was a junk dealer in a Canadian city. He kept a Bible open on his shelves; during intervals of business, he pondered the Book of God. His Bible became black from handling in such surroundings, but I have little doubt his soul became correspondingly white. No economy pays as does the economy of time, but there is no way of economizing time so thriftily as putting wasted moments into the study of or meditation on the Word of God.

HOW TO WITNESS TO ANYONE

INTRODUCTION

In a compelling passage of Scripture in the book of Matthew, Jesus told His disciples:

> *The harvest truly is plenteous, but the labourers are few; pray ye therefore the Lord of the harvest, that he will send forth labourers into his harvest.* (Matthew 9:37–38)

When Christians answer the call to labor in God's field of harvest, they may be sent across the street to witness to a neighbor or across the ocean to a different culture. These workers must be prepared to answer a variety of questions and arguments when they confront people with the truth about heaven, hell, and eternity.

Through His Word, God has revealed Himself and given the answer to every doubt and every need in the heart of man. *How to Witness to Anyone* conveniently groups Scriptures according to topics, providing the Christian laborer with a valuable tool for ministry. The subjects and Scriptures correspond to R. A. Torrey's larger and more detailed work *How to Bring Men to Christ.*

Study these Scriptures and prepare your heart to testify about the Lord Jesus Christ. Then, when someone with whom you are sharing the gospel says, "I can't give up my evil ways" or "I will lose my friends if I come to Christ," you can reply using God's own Word. Therefore, prepare yourself, and then allow God to use you in the glorious ministry of reconciliation.

CHAPTER 1

YOU CAN BE A SOULWINNER

Certain requirements must be fulfilled for real success in leading lost souls to Christ. Fortunately, these are few and simple, and anyone can meet them.

First, be a born-again believer. If you desire to bring others to Christ, you must turn away from all sin, worldliness, and selfishness, allowing Jesus to be Lord over your thoughts, purposes, and actions.

Second, truly love others and long for their salvation. If you have no love for other souls, your efforts will be mechanical and powerless. But if you, like Paul, have great heaviness and continual pain in your heart for the unsaved (see Romans 9:2), the earnestness in your tone and manner will impress even the most uninterested person. Furthermore, you will be watching for opportunities to tell people about Jesus.

Third, have a working knowledge of the Bible. The Word of God is the sword of the Spirit (see Ephesians 6:17), which God uses to convict people of sin, to reveal Christ, and to regenerate the lost. You must use the Bible to bring people to Christ.

Fourth, pray frequently. Pray about whom you should speak to and what you should say. Pray that you will speak powerfully.

Fifth, be baptized in the Holy Spirit. After Jesus gave His disciples the Great Commission, He told them,

> But ye shall receive power, after that the Holy Ghost is come upon you: and ye shall be witnesses unto me both in Jerusalem, and in all Judaea, and in Samaria, and unto the uttermost part of the earth. (Acts 1:8)

The next two chapters contain promises from God's Word that explain His plan of salvation. Several chapters that follow give specific verses to answer the many objections that unbelievers have to God's plan. Then, there are chapters containing verses to help the new believer to become stronger and to weather difficult times. The final chapter gives valuable hints for you, the soulwinner.

CHAPTER 2

THE PROMISE OF SALVATION

1. ALL HAVE SINNED

There is no difference: for all have sinned, and come short of the glory of God. (Romans 3:22–23)

If we say that we have no sin, we deceive ourselves, and the truth is not in us....If we say that we have not sinned, we make him a liar, and his word is not in us. (1 John 1:8, 10)

Thou shalt love the Lord thy God with all thy heart, and with all thy soul, and with all thy mind. This is the first and great commandment. (Matthew 22:37–38)

If thou, LORD, shouldest mark iniquities, O Lord, who shall stand? (Psalm 130:3)

2. THE CONSEQUENCES OF SIN AND UNBELIEF

But the wicked are like the troubled sea, when it cannot rest, whose waters cast up mire and dirt. There is no peace, saith my God, to the wicked. (Isaiah 57:20–21)

Jesus answered them, Verily, verily, I say unto you, Whosoever committeth sin is the servant of sin. (John 8:34)

For as many as are of the works of the law are under the curse: for it is written, Cursed is every one that continueth not in all things which are written in the book of the law to do them. (Galatians 3:10)

He that believeth on the Son hath everlasting life: and he that believeth not the Son shall not see life; but the wrath of God abideth on him.   (John 3:36)

He that believeth on him is not condemned: but he that believeth not is condemned already, because he hath not believed in the name of the only begotten Son of God.   (John 3:18)

For the wages of sin is death; but the gift of God is eternal life through Jesus Christ our Lord.   (Romans 6:23)

The Lord Jesus shall be revealed from heaven with his mighty angels, in flaming fire taking vengeance on them that know not God, and that obey not the gospel of our Lord Jesus Christ: who shall be punished with everlasting destruction from the presence of the Lord, and from the glory of his power.   (2 Thessalonians 1:7–9)

Ye shall die in your sins: for if ye believe not that I am he, ye shall die in your sins.   (John 8:24)

But the fearful, and unbelieving, and the abominable, and murderers, and whoremongers, and sorcerers, and idolaters, and all liars, shall have their part in the lake which burneth with fire and brimstone: which is the second death.   (Revelation 21:8)

He that despised Moses' law died without mercy under two or three witnesses: of how much sorer punishment, suppose ye, shall he be thought worthy, who hath trodden under foot the Son of God, and hath counted the blood of the covenant, wherewith he was sanctified, an unholy thing, and hath done despite unto the Spirit of grace?
                                                  (Hebrews 10:28–29)

3. GOD'S LOVE FOR MAN

For God so loved the world, that he gave his only begotten Son, that whosoever believeth in him should not perish, but have everlasting life.   (John 3:16)

For when we were yet without strength, in due time Christ died for the ungodly. …God commendeth his love toward us, in that, while we were yet sinners, Christ died for us. (Romans 5:6, 8)

But he was wounded for our transgressions, he was bruised for our iniquities: the chastisement of our peace was upon him; and with his stripes we are healed. All we like sheep have gone astray; we have turned every one to his own way; and the LORD *hath laid on him the iniquity of us all.* (Isaiah 53:5–6)

And being in an agony he prayed more earnestly: and his sweat was as it were great drops of blood falling down to the ground. (Luke 22:44)

And about the ninth hour Jesus cried with a loud voice, saying, Eli, Eli, lama sabachthani? That is to say, My God, my God, why hast thou forsaken me? (Matthew 27:46)

Christ hath redeemed us from the curse of the law, being made a curse for us: for it is written, Cursed is every one that hangeth on a tree. (Galatians 3:13)

Forasmuch as ye know that ye were not redeemed with corruptible things, as silver and gold, from your vain conversation received by tradition from your fathers; but with the precious blood of Christ, as of a lamb without blemish and without spot. (1 Peter 1:18–19)

CHAPTER 3

DEALING WITH THE OPENHEARTED

1. JESUS—OUR SIN-BEARER

All we like sheep have gone astray; we have turned every one to his own way; and the LORD hath laid on him the iniquity of us all.

(Isaiah 53:6)

Who his own self bare our sins in his own body on the tree, that we, being dead to sins, should live unto righteousness: by whose stripes ye were healed. (1 Peter 2:24)

Herein is love, not that we loved God, but that he loved us, and sent his Son to be the propitiation for our sins. (1 John 4:10)

And he is the propitiation for our sins: and not for ours only, but also for the sins of the whole world. (1 John 2:2)

For it pleased the Father that in him should all fulness dwell; and, having made peace through the blood of his cross, by him to reconcile all things unto himself; by him, I say, whether they be things in earth, or things in heaven. (Colossians 1:19–20)

In whom we have redemption through his blood, the forgiveness of sins, according to the riches of his grace. (Ephesians 1:7)

For when we were yet without strength, in due time Christ died for the ungodly. For scarcely for a righteous man will one die: yet peradventure for a good man some would even dare to die. But God commendeth his love toward us, in that, while we were yet sinners, Christ died for us. Much more then, being now justified by his blood, we shall be saved from wrath through him. For if, when we were enemies, we were reconciled to God by the death of his Son, much more, being reconciled, we shall be saved by his life. And not only so, but we also joy in God through our Lord Jesus Christ, by whom we have now received the atonement. (Romans 5:6–11)

2. JESUS—OUR RISEN SAVIOR

Moreover, brethren, I declare unto you the gospel which I preached unto you, which also ye have received, and wherein ye stand; by which also ye are saved, if ye keep in memory what I preached unto you, unless ye have believed in vain. For I delivered unto you first of all that which I also received, how that Christ died for our sins according to the scriptures; and that he was buried, and that he rose again the third day according to the scriptures. (1 Corinthians 15:1–4)

And she shall bring forth a son, and thou shalt call his name JESUS: for he shall save his people from their sins. (Matthew 1:21)

Now if I do that I would not, it is no more I that do it, but sin that dwelleth in me. I find then a law, that, when I would do good, evil is present with me. For I delight in the law of God after the inward man: but I see another law in my members, warring against the law of my mind, and bringing me into captivity to the law of sin which is in my members. O wretched man that I am! Who shall deliver me from the body of this death? I thank God through Jesus Christ our Lord. (Romans 7:20–25)

[He] is able to keep you from falling, and to present you faultless before the presence of his glory with exceeding joy. (Jude 24)

[We] are kept by the power of God through faith unto salvation ready to be revealed in the last time. (1 Peter 1:5)

3. JESUS—OUR EVER LIVING INTERCESSOR

My little children, these things write I unto you, that ye sin not. And if any man sin, we have an advocate with the Father, Jesus Christ the righteous. (1 John 2:1)

Who is he that condemneth? It is Christ that died, yea rather, that is risen again, who is even at the right hand of God, who also maketh intercession for us.   (Romans 8:34)

Wherefore he is able also to save them to the uttermost that come unto God by him, seeing he ever liveth to make intercession for them.
                                   (Hebrews 7:25)

4. BELIEVING, RECEIVING, AND CONFESSING JESUS

But as many as received him, to them gave he power to become the sons of God, even to them that believe on his name.   (John 1:12)

Believe on the Lord Jesus Christ, and thou shalt be saved, and thy house.   (Acts 16:31)

For God so loved the world, that he gave his only begotten Son, that whosoever believeth in him should not perish, but have everlasting life.   (John 3:16)

Look unto me, and be ye saved, all the ends of the earth: for I am God, and there is none else.   (Isaiah 45:22)

If thou shalt confess with thy mouth the Lord Jesus, and shalt believe in thine heart that God hath raised him from the dead, thou shalt be saved. For with the heart man believeth unto righteousness; and with the mouth confession is made unto salvation.   (Romans 10:9–10)

He that believeth on the Son hath everlasting life: and he that believeth not the Son shall not see life; but the wrath of God abideth on him.   (John 3:36)

To him give all the prophets witness, that through his name whosoever believeth in him shall receive remission of sins.   (Acts 10:43)

And by him all that believe are justified from all things, from which ye could not be justified by the law of Moses.   (Acts 13:39)

CHAPTER 4

DEALING WITH DIFFICULTIES

1. I AM TOO GREAT A SINNER.

This is a faithful saying, and worthy of all acceptation, that Christ Jesus came into the world to save sinners; of whom I am chief.
(1 Timothy 1:15)

For when we were yet without strength, in due time Christ died for the ungodly....God commendeth his love toward us, in that, while we were yet sinners, Christ died for us. (Romans 5:6, 8)

Come now, and let us reason together, saith the LORD: though your sins be as scarlet, they shall be as white as snow; though they be red like crimson, they shall be as wool. (Isaiah 1:18)

To him give all the prophets witness, that through his name whosoever believeth in him shall receive remission of sins. (Acts 10:43)

For the Son of man is come to seek and to save that which was lost.
(Luke 19:10)

All that the Father giveth me shall come to me; and him that cometh to me I will in no wise cast out. (John 6:37)

2. I AM AFRAID OF FAILURE.

And I give unto them eternal life; and they shall never perish, neither shall any man pluck them out of my hand. My Father, which gave them me, is greater than all; and no man is able to pluck them out of my Father's hand. (John 10:28–29)

Fear thou not; for I am with thee: be not dismayed; for I am thy God: I will strengthen thee; yea, I will help thee; yea, I will uphold thee with the right hand of my righteousness....For I the LORD thy God will hold thy right hand, saying unto thee, Fear not; I will help thee.

(Isaiah 41:10, 13)

[We] are kept by the power of God through faith unto salvation ready to be revealed in the last time. (1 Peter 1:5)

For the which cause I also suffer these things: nevertheless I am not ashamed: for I know whom I have believed, and am persuaded that he is able to keep that which I have committed unto him against that day. (2 Timothy 1:12)

Be strong and courageous, be not afraid nor dismayed for the king of Assyria, nor for all the multitude that is with him: for there be more with us than with him: with him is an arm of flesh; but with us is the LORD our God to help us, and to fight our battles. (2 Chronicles 32:7–8)

Who art thou that judgest another man's servant? To his own master he standeth or falleth. Yea, he shall be holden up: for God is able to make him stand. (Romans 14:4)

But the Lord is faithful, who shall stablish you, and keep you from evil. (2 Thessalonians 3:3)

There hath no temptation taken you but such as is common to man: but God is faithful, who will not suffer you to be tempted above that ye are able; but will with the temptation also make a way to escape, that ye may be able to bear it. (1 Corinthians 10:13)

3. I AM TOO WEAK.

And he said unto me, My grace is sufficient for thee: for my strength is made perfect in weakness. Most gladly therefore will I rather glory in my infirmities, that the power of Christ may rest upon me. Therefore I take pleasure in infirmities, in reproaches, in necessities,

in persecutions, in distresses for Christ's sake: for when I am weak,
then am I strong. (2 Corinthians 12:9–10)

I can do all things through Christ which strengtheneth me.
(Philippians 4:13)

For what the law could not do, in that it was weak through the flesh,
God sending his own Son in the likeness of sinful flesh, and for sin,
condemned sin in the flesh: that the righteousness of the law might be
fulfilled in us, who walk not after the flesh, but after the Spirit.
(Romans 8:3–4)

He giveth power to the faint; and to them that have no might he
increaseth strength. Even the youths shall faint and be weary, and the
young men shall utterly fall: but they that wait upon the LORD *shall*
renew their strength; they shall mount up with wings as eagles; they
shall run, and not be weary; and they shall walk, and not faint.
(Isaiah 40:29–31)

Thy word have I hid in mine heart, that I might not sin against thee.
(Psalm 119:11)

For whatsoever is born of God overcometh the world: and this is the
victory that overcometh the world, even our faith. (1 John 5:4)

Be sober, be vigilant; because your adversary the devil, as a roaring
lion, walketh about, seeking whom he may devour: whom resist sted-
fast in the faith, knowing that the same afflictions are accomplished
in your brethren that are in the world. But the God of all grace, who
hath called us unto his eternal glory by Christ Jesus, after that ye have
suffered a while, make you perfect, stablish, strengthen, settle you.
(1 Peter 5:8–10)

4. I CANNOT GIVE UP MY EVIL WAYS AND BAD HABITS.

Be not deceived; God is not mocked: for whatsoever a man soweth,
that shall he also reap. For he that soweth to his flesh shall of the flesh

reap corruption; but he that soweth to the Spirit shall of the Spirit reap life everlasting. (Galatians 6:7–8)

I can do all things through Christ which strengtheneth me.
(Philippians 4:13)

If the Son therefore shall make you free, ye shall be free indeed.
(John 8:36)

5. I WILL BE PERSECUTED IF I BECOME A CHRISTIAN.

Yea, and all that will live godly in Christ Jesus shall suffer persecution. (2 Timothy 3:12)

Blessed are they which are persecuted for righteousness' sake: for theirs is the kingdom of heaven. Blessed are ye, when men shall revile you, and persecute you, and shall say all manner of evil against you falsely, for my sake. Rejoice, and be exceeding glad: for great is your reward in heaven: for so persecuted they the prophets which were before you.
(Matthew 5:10–12)

For whosoever will save his life shall lose it; but whosoever shall lose his life for my sake and the gospel's, the same shall save it....Whosoever therefore shall be ashamed of me and of my words in this adulterous and sinful generation; of him also shall the Son of man be ashamed, when he cometh in the glory of his Father with the holy angels.
(Mark 8:35, 38)

For I reckon that the sufferings of this present time are not worthy to be compared with the glory which shall be revealed in us. (Romans 8:18)

Continue in the faith...[for] we must through much tribulation enter into the kingdom of God. (Acts 14:22)

And when they had called the apostles, and beaten them, they commanded that they should not speak in the name of Jesus, and let them go. And they departed from the presence of the council, rejoicing that they were counted worthy to suffer shame for his name.

(Acts 5:40–41)

If we suffer, we shall also reign with him: if we deny him, he also will deny us. (2 Timothy 2:12)

Looking unto Jesus the author and finisher of our faith; who for the joy that was set before him endured the cross, despising the shame, and is set down at the right hand of the throne of God. For consider him that endured such contradiction of sinners against himself, lest ye be wearied and faint in your minds. (Hebrews 12:2–3)

For what glory is it, if, when ye be buffeted for your faults, ye shall take it patiently? but if, when ye do well, and suffer for it, ye take it patiently, this is acceptable with God. For even hereunto were ye called: because Christ also suffered for us, leaving us an example, that ye should follow his steps. (1 Peter 2:20–21)

6. I WILL LOSE MY FRIENDS.

The fear of man bringeth a snare: but whoso putteth his trust in the LORD *shall be safe.* (Proverbs 29:25)

He that walketh with wise men shall be wise: but a companion of fools shall be destroyed. (Proverbs 13:20)

Blessed is the man that walketh not in the counsel of the ungodly, nor standeth in the way of sinners, nor sitteth in the seat of the scornful. But his delight is in the law of the LORD*; and in his law doth he meditate day and night.* (Psalm 1:1–2)

That which we have seen and heard declare we unto you, that ye also may have fellowship with us: and truly our fellowship is with the Father, and with his Son Jesus Christ. (1 John 1:3)

Ye adulterers and adulteresses, know ye not that the friendship of the world is enmity with God? Whosoever therefore will be a friend of the world is the enemy of God. (James 4:4)

7. I HAVE TOO MUCH TO GIVE UP.

For what shall it profit a man, if he shall gain the whole world, and lose his own soul? (Mark 8:36)

But seek ye first the kingdom of God, and his righteousness; and all these things shall be added unto you. (Matthew 6:33)

For the LORD God is a sun and shield: the LORD will give grace and glory: no good thing will he withhold from them that walk uprightly. (Psalm 84:11)

He that spared not his own Son, but delivered him up for us all, how shall he not with him also freely give us all things? (Romans 8:32)

Love not the world, neither the things that are in the world. If any man love the world, the love of the Father is not in him. For all that is in the world, the lust of the flesh, and the lust of the eyes, and the pride of life, is not of the Father, but is of the world. And the world passeth away, and the lust thereof: but he that doeth the will of God abideth for ever. (1 John 2:15–17)

By faith Moses, when he was come to years, refused to be called the son of Pharaoh's daughter; choosing rather to suffer affliction with the people of God, than to enjoy the pleasures of sin for a season; esteeming the reproach of Christ greater riches than the treasures in Egypt: for he had respect unto the recompense of the reward. (Hebrews 11:24–26)

But what things were gain to me, those I counted loss for Christ. Yea doubtless, and I count all things but loss for the excellency of the knowledge of Christ Jesus my Lord: for whom I have suffered the loss of all things, and do count them but dung, that I may win Christ. (Philippians 3:7–8)

The ground of a certain rich man brought forth plentifully: and he thought within himself, saying, What shall I do, because I have no room where to bestow my fruits? And he said, This will I do: I will pull down my barns, and build greater; and there will I bestow all my fruits and my goods. And I will say to my soul, Soul, thou hast much goods laid up for many years; take thine ease, eat, drink, and be merry. But God said unto him, Thou fool, this night thy soul shall be required of thee: then whose shall those things be, which thou hast provided? So is he that layeth up treasure for himself, and is not rich toward God. (Luke 12:16–21)

For my yoke is easy, and my burden is light. (Matthew 11:30)

8. I DON'T HAVE THE RIGHT FEELINGS.

God does not demand that we feel sorry for our sins, but that we turn from sin and receive Christ. For with the heart man believeth unto righteousness; and with the mouth confession is made unto salvation. (Romans 10:10)

Let the wicked forsake his way, and the unrighteous man his thoughts: and let him return unto the LORD, and he will have mercy upon him; and to our God, for he will abundantly pardon. (Isaiah 55:7)

But as many as received him, to them gave he power to become the sons of God, even to them that believe on his name. (John 1:12)

Believe on the Lord Jesus Christ, and thou shalt be saved, and thy house. (Acts 16:31)

9. I AM SEEKING CHRIST BUT CANNOT FIND HIM.

And ye shall seek me, and find me, when ye shall search for me with all your heart. (Jeremiah 29:13)

What man of you, having an hundred sheep, if he lose one of them, doth not leave the ninety and nine in the wilderness, and go after that which is lost, until he find it? And when he hath found it, he layeth it on his shoulders, rejoicing. And when he cometh home, he calleth together his friends and neighbours, saying unto them, Rejoice with me; for I have found my sheep which was lost. I say unto you, that likewise joy shall be in heaven over one sinner that repenteth, more than over ninety and nine just persons, which need no repentance. Either what woman having ten pieces of silver, if she lose one piece, doth not light a candle, and sweep the house, and seek diligently till she find it? And when she hath found it, she calleth her friends and her neighbours together, saying, Rejoice with me; for I have found the piece which I had lost. Likewise, I say unto you, there is joy in the presence of the angels of God over one sinner that repenteth.

(Luke 15:4–10)

For the Son of man is come to seek and to save that which was lost.

(Luke 19:10)

Also read the passages under "Jesus—Our Sin-Bearer."

10. MY HEART IS TOO HARD.

A new heart also will I give you, and a new spirit will I put within you: and I will take away the stony heart out of your flesh, and I will give you an heart of flesh. And I will put my spirit within you, and cause you to walk in my statutes, and ye shall keep my judgments, and do them.   (Ezekiel 36:26–27)

11. GOD WILL NOT RECEIVE ME.

All that the Father giveth me shall come to me; and him that cometh to me I will in no wise cast out.   (John 6:37)

For whosoever shall call upon the name of the Lord shall be saved.

(Romans 10:13)

Manasseh was twelve years old when he began to reign, and he reigned fifty and five years in Jerusalem: but did that which was evil in the sight of the LORD, *like unto the abominations of the heathen, whom the* LORD *had cast out before the children of Israel. ...And the* LORD *spake to Manasseh, and to his people: but they would not hearken. Wherefore the* LORD *brought upon them the captains of the host of the king of Assyria, which took Manasseh among the thorns, and bound him with fetters, and carried him to Babylon. And when he was in affliction, he besought the* LORD *his God, and humbled himself greatly before the God of his fathers, and prayed unto him: and he was entreated of him, and heard his supplication, and brought him again to Jerusalem into his kingdom. Then Manasseh knew that the* LORD *he was God.* (2 Chronicles 33:1–2, 10–13)

12. I HAVE COMMITTED THE UNPARDONABLE SIN.

What is the unpardonable sin?

Wherefore I say unto you, All manner of sin and blasphemy shall be forgiven unto men: but the blasphemy against the Holy Ghost shall not be forgiven unto men. And whosoever speaketh a word against the Son of man, it shall be forgiven him: but whosoever speaketh against the Holy Ghost, it shall not be forgiven him, neither in this world, neither in the world to come. (Matthew 12:31–32)

For it is impossible for those who were once enlightened, and have tasted of the heavenly gift, and were made partakers of the Holy Ghost, and have tasted the good word of God, and the powers of the world to come, if they shall fall away, to renew them again unto repentance; seeing they crucify to themselves the Son of God afresh, and put him to an open shame. (Hebrews 6:4–6)

This passage describes one who renounces Christianity and returns to the things of this world, not one who merely falls into sin, even deep sin, as Peter did.

13. IT IS TOO LATE.

When thou art in tribulation, and all these things are come upon thee, even in the latter days, if thou turn to the LORD *thy God, and shalt be obedient unto his voice; (for the* LORD *thy God is a merciful God;) he will not forsake thee, neither destroy thee, nor forget the covenant of thy fathers which he sware unto them.* (Deuteronomy 4:30–31)

The Lord is not slack concerning his promise, as some men count slackness; but is longsuffering to us-ward, not willing that any should perish, but that all should come to repentance. (2 Peter 3:9)

And the Spirit and the bride say, Come. And let him that heareth say, Come. And let him that is athirst come. And whosoever will, let him take the water of life freely. (Revelation 22:17)

14. I MUST BECOME A BETTER PERSON FIRST.

They that be whole need not a physician, but they that are sick. But go ye and learn what that meaneth, I will have mercy, and not sacrifice: for I am not come to call the righteous, but sinners to repentance.
(Matthew 9:12–13)

I will arise and go to my father, and will say unto him, Father, I have sinned against heaven, and before thee. …And he arose, and came to his father. But when he was yet a great way off, his father saw him, and had compassion, and ran, and fell on his neck, and kissed him. And the son said unto him, Father, I have sinned against heaven, and in thy sight, and am no more worthy to be called thy son. But the father said to his servants, Bring forth the best robe, and put it on him; and put a ring on his hand, and shoes on his feet: and bring hither the fatted calf, and kill it; and let us eat, and be merry: for this my son was dead, and is alive again; he was lost, and is found.
(Luke 15:18, 20–24)

Two men went up into the temple to pray; the one a Pharisee, and the other a publican. The Pharisee stood and prayed thus with himself, God, I thank thee, that I am not as other men are, extortioners, unjust, adulterers, or even as this publican. I fast twice in the week, I give tithes of all that I possess. And the publican, standing afar off, would not lift up so much as his eyes unto heaven, but smote upon his breast, saying, God be merciful to me a sinner. I tell you, this man went down to his house justified rather than the other: for every one that exalteth himself shall be abased; and he that humbleth himself shall be exalted.
(Luke 18:10–14)

I have blotted out, as a thick cloud, thy transgressions, and, as a cloud, thy sins: return unto me; for I have redeemed thee.
(Isaiah 44:22)

CHAPTER 5

DEALING WITH THE SELF-RIGHTEOUS

1. I'M NO WORSE THAN ANYBODY ELSE.

Knowing that a man is not justified by the works of the law, but by the faith of Jesus Christ, even we have believed in Jesus Christ, that we might be justified by the faith of Christ, and not by the works of the law: for by the works of the law shall no flesh be justified. (Galatians 2:16)

Now we know that what things soever the law saith, it saith to them who are under the law: that every mouth may be stopped, and all the world may become guilty before God. Therefore by the deeds of the law there shall no flesh be justified in his sight: for by the law is the knowledge of sin. (Romans 3:19–20)

For as many as are of the works of the law are under the curse: for it is written, Cursed is every one that continueth not in all things which are written in the book of the law to do them. (Galatians 3:10)

For whosoever shall keep the whole law, and yet offend in one point, he is guilty of all. (James 2:10)

Except your righteousness shall exceed the righteousness of the scribes and Pharisees, ye shall in no case enter into the kingdom of heaven. (Matthew 5:20)

And he said unto them, Ye are they which justify yourselves before men; but God knoweth your hearts: for that which is highly esteemed among men is abomination in the sight of God. (Luke 16:15)

God shall judge the secrets of men by Jesus Christ according to my gospel. (Romans 2:16)

Man looketh on the outward appearance, but the LORD *looketh on the heart.* (1 Samuel 16:7)

But without faith it is impossible to please him: for he that cometh to God must believe that he is, and that he is a rewarder of them that diligently seek him. (Hebrews 11:6)

He that despised Moses' law died without mercy under two or three witnesses: of how much sorer punishment, suppose ye, shall he be thought worthy, who hath trodden under foot the Son of God, and hath counted the blood of the covenant, wherewith he was sanctified, an unholy thing, and hath done despite unto the Spirit of grace? (Hebrews 10:28–29)

2. GOD IS TOO GOOD TO DAMN ANYONE.

Or despisest thou the riches of his goodness and forbearance and long-suffering; not knowing that the goodness of God leadeth thee to repentance? But after thy hardness and impenitent heart treasurest up unto thyself wrath against the day of wrath and revelation of the righteous judgment of God. (Romans 2:4–5)

If ye believe not that I am he, ye shall die in your sins. (John 8:24)

The Lord is not slack concerning his promise, as some men count slackness; but is longsuffering to us-ward, not willing that any should perish, but that all should come to repentance. But the day of the Lord will come as a thief in the night; in the which the heavens shall pass away with a great noise, and the elements shall melt with fervent heat, the earth also and the works that are therein shall be burned up. Seeing then that all these things shall be dissolved, what manner of persons ought ye to be in all holy conversation and godliness? (2 Peter 3:9–11)

I have no pleasure in the death of the wicked; but that the wicked turn from his way and live: turn ye, turn ye from your evil ways; for why will ye die, O house of Israel? (Ezekiel 33:11)

For if God spared not the angels that sinned, but cast them down to hell, and delivered them into chains of darkness, to be reserved unto judgment; and spared not the old world, but saved Noah the eighth person, a preacher of righteousness, bringing in the flood upon the world of the ungodly; and turning the cities of Sodom and Gomorrha into ashes condemned them with an overthrow, making them an ensample unto those that after should live ungodly…the Lord knoweth how to deliver the godly out of temptations, and to reserve the unjust unto the day of judgment to be punished.   (2 Peter 2:4–6, 9)

Except ye repent, ye shall all likewise perish.   (Luke 13:3)

He that believeth on him is not condemned: but he that believeth not is condemned already, because he hath not believed in the name of the only begotten Son of God.   (John 3:18)

3. I'M TRYING TO BE A GOOD CHRISTIAN.

We are saved by trusting what Jesus has done and will do, not by any effort of our own.

For all have sinned, and come short of the glory of God; being justified freely by his grace through the redemption that is in Christ Jesus: whom God hath set forth to be a propitiation through faith in his blood.   (Romans 3:23–25)

For what saith the scripture? Abraham believed God, and it was counted unto him for righteousness. Now to him that worketh is the reward not reckoned of grace, but of debt. But to him that worketh not, but believeth on him that justified the ungodly, his faith is counted for righteousness.   (Romans 4:3–5)

But as many as received him, to them gave he power to become the sons of God, even to them that believe on his name.   (John 1:12)

Behold, God is my salvation; I will trust, and not be afraid: for the LORD JEHOVAH *is my strength and my song; he also is become my salvation.*   (Isaiah 12:2)

4. I FEEL THAT I AM SAVED.

There is a way which seemeth right unto a man, but the end thereof are the ways of death. (Proverbs 14:12)

He that believeth on the Son hath everlasting life: and he that believeth not the Son shall not see life; but the wrath of God abideth on him. (John 3:36)

5. I BELONG TO A CHURCH.

Follow peace with all men, and holiness, without which no man shall see the Lord. (Hebrews 12:14)

Know ye not that the unrighteous shall not inherit the kingdom of God? Be not deceived: neither fornicators, nor idolaters, nor adulterers, nor effeminate, nor abusers of themselves with mankind, nor thieves, nor covetous, nor drunkards, nor revilers, nor extortioners, shall inherit the kingdom of God. (1 Corinthians 6:9–10)

They profess that they know God; but in works they deny him, being abominable, and disobedient, and unto every good work reprobate. (Titus 1:16)

What doth it profit, my brethren, though a man say he hath faith, and have not works? Can faith save him? (James 2:14)

Jesus answered and said unto him, Verily, verily, I say unto thee, Except a man be born again, he cannot see the kingdom of God. (John 3:3)

If ye know that he is righteous, ye know that every one that doeth righteousness is born of him. (1 John 2:29)

But the fearful, and unbelieving, and the abominable, and murderers, and whoremongers, and sorcerers, and idolaters, and all liars, shall have their part in the lake which burneth with fire and brimstone: which is the second death. (Revelation 21:8)

CHAPTER 6

DEALING WITH THE UNCERTAIN AND WITH BACKSLIDERS

1. HOW CAN I KNOW I AM SAVED?

These things have I written unto you that believe on the name of the Son of God; that ye may know that ye have eternal life.

(1 John 5:13)

Verily, verily, I say unto you, He that heareth my word, and believeth on him that sent me, hath everlasting life, and shall not come into condemnation; but is passed from death unto life. (John 5:24)

And this is the record, that God hath given to us eternal life, and this life is in his Son. He that hath the Son hath life; and he that hath not the Son of God hath not life. (1 John 5:11–12)

I am the light of the world: he that followeth me shall not walk in darkness, but shall have the light of life. (John 8:12)

Let the wicked forsake his way, and the unrighteous man his thoughts: and let him return unto the Lord, and he will have mercy upon him; and to our God, for he will abundantly pardon. (Isaiah 55:7)

2. I DO NOT CARE ABOUT SERVING GOD ANYMORE.

What iniquity have your fathers found in me, that they are gone far from me, and have walked after vanity, and are become vain? ...For my people have committed two evils; they have forsaken me the fountain of living waters, and hewed them out cisterns, broken cisterns, that can hold no water. ...Thine own wickedness shall correct thee, and thy backslidings shall reprove thee: know therefore and see that it is an evil thing and bitter, that thou hast forsaken the Lord thy God,

and that my fear is not in thee, saith the Lord GOD *of hosts.*
(Jeremiah 2:5, 13, 19)

I have overthrown some of you, as God overthrew Sodom and Gomorrah, and ye were as a firebrand plucked out of the burning: yet have ye not returned unto me, saith the LORD. *Therefore thus will I do unto thee, O Israel: and because I will do this unto thee, prepare to meet thy God, O Israel.*
(Amos 4:11–12)

The backslider in heart shall be filled with his own ways: and a good man shall be satisfied from himself.
(Proverbs 14:14)

3. I WANT TO COME BACK TO THE LORD.

Go and proclaim these words toward the north, and say, Return, thou backsliding Israel, saith the LORD; *and I will not cause mine anger to fall upon you: for I am merciful, saith the* LORD, *and I will not keep anger for ever. Only acknowledge thine iniquity, that thou hast transgressed against the* LORD *thy God, and hast scattered thy ways to the strangers under every green tree, and ye have not obeyed my voice, saith the* LORD. …*Return, ye backsliding children, and I will heal your backslidings. Behold, we come unto thee; for thou art the* LORD *our God.*
(Jeremiah 3:12–13, 22)

O Israel, return unto the LORD *thy God; for thou hast fallen by thine iniquity. Take with you words, and turn to the* LORD: *say unto him, Take away all iniquity, and receive us graciously: so will we render the calves of our lips Asshur shall not save us; we will not ride upon horses: neither will we say any more to the work of our hands, Ye are our gods: for in thee the fatherless findeth mercy. I will heal their backsliding, I will love them freely: for mine anger is turned away from him.*
(Hosea 14:1–4)

But thou hast not called upon me, O Jacob; but thou hast been weary of me, O Israel. …Thou hast bought me no sweet cane with money, neither hast thou filled me with the fat of thy sacrifices: but thou hast made me to serve with thy sins, thou hast wearied me with thine iniquities. I, even I, am he that blotteth out thy transgressions for mine own sake, and will not remember thy sins.

(Isaiah 43:22, 24–25)

I have blotted out, as a thick cloud, thy transgressions, and, as a cloud, thy sins: return unto me; for I have redeemed thee.

(Isaiah 44:22)

For I know the thoughts that I think toward you, saith the LORD, *thoughts of peace, and not of evil, to give you an expected end. Then shall ye call upon me, and ye shall go and pray unto me, and I will hearken unto you. And ye shall seek me, and find me, when ye shall search for me with all your heart.* (Jeremiah 29:11–13)

And there ye shall serve gods, the work of men's hands, wood and stone, which neither see, nor hear, nor eat, nor smell. But if from thence thou shalt seek the LORD *thy God, thou shalt find him, if thou seek him with all thy heart and with all thy soul. When thou art in tribulation, and all these things are come upon thee, even in the latter days, if thou turn to the* LORD *thy God, and shalt be obedient unto his voice; (for the* LORD *thy God is a merciful God;) he will not forsake thee, neither destroy thee, nor forget the covenant of thy fathers which he sware unto them.* (Deuteronomy 4:28–31)

If my people, which are called by my name, shall humble themselves, and pray, and seek my face, and turn from their wicked ways; then will I hear from heaven, and will forgive their sin, and will heal their land. (2 Chronicles 7:14)

If we confess our sins, he is faithful and just to forgive us our sins, and to cleanse us from all unrighteousness. (1 John 1:9)

But when they in their trouble did turn unto the LORD *God of Israel, and sought him, he was found of them.* (2 Chronicles 15:4)

And not many days after the younger son gathered all together, and took his journey into a far country, and there wasted his substance with riotous living. And when he had spent all, there arose a mighty famine in that land; and he began to be in want. And he went and joined himself to a citizen of that country; and he sent him into his fields to feed swine. And he would fain have filled his belly with the husks that the swine did eat: and no man gave unto him. And when he came to himself, he said, How many hired servants of my father's have bread enough and to spare, and I perish with hunger! I will arise and go to my father, and will say unto him, Father, I have sinned against heaven, and before thee, and am no more worthy to be called thy son: make me as one of thy hired servants. And he arose, and came to his father. But when he was yet a great way off, his father saw him, and had compassion, and ran, and fell on his neck, and kissed him. And the son said unto him, Father, I have sinned against heaven, and in thy sight, and am no more worthy to be called thy son. But the father said to his servants, Bring forth the best robe, and put it on him; and put a ring on his hand, and shoes on his feet: and bring hither the fatted calf, and kill it; and let us eat, and be merry: for this my son was dead, and is alive again; he was lost, and is found. And they began to be merry.   (Luke 15:13–24)

CHAPTER 7

DEALING WITH SKEPTICS

1. THE BIBLE AND GOD'S PLAN OF SALVATION SEEM FOOLISH TO ME.

For the preaching of the cross is to them that perish foolishness; but unto us which are saved it is the power of God. (1 Corinthians 1:18)

But if our gospel be hid, it is hid to them that are lost: in whom the god of this world hath blinded the minds of them which believe not, lest the light of the glorious gospel of Christ, who is the image of God, should shine unto them. (2 Corinthians 4:3–4)

The Lord Jesus shall be revealed from heaven with his mighty angels, in flaming fire taking vengeance on them that know not God, and that obey not the gospel of our Lord Jesus Christ. (2 Thessalonians 1:7–8)

Then shall that Wicked be revealed…even him, whose coming is after the working of Satan with all power and signs and lying wonders, and with all deceivableness of unrighteousness in them that perish; because they received not the love of the truth, that they might be saved. And for this cause God shall send them strong delusion, that they should believe a lie: that they all might be damned who believed not the truth, but had pleasure in unrighteousness. (2 Thessalonians 2:8–12)

He that believeth and is baptized shall be saved; but he that believeth not shall be damned. (Mark 16:16)

2. I HAVE TRIED, BUT I CANNOT BELIEVE.

If any man will do his will, he shall know of the doctrine, whether it be of God, or whether I speak of myself. (John 7:17)

But the natural man receiveth not the things of the Spirit of God: for they are foolishness unto him: neither can he know them, because they are spiritually discerned.   (1 Corinthians 2:14)

Philip findeth Nathanael, and saith unto him, We have found him, of whom Moses in the law, and the prophets, did write, Jesus of Nazareth, the son of Joseph. And Nathanael said unto him, Can there any good thing come out of Nazareth? Philip saith unto him, Come and see. Jesus saw Nathanael coming to him, and saith of him, Behold an Israelite indeed, in whom is no guile! Nathanael saith unto him, Whence knowest thou me? Jesus answered and said unto him, Before that Philip called thee, when thou wast under the fig tree, I saw thee. Nathanael answered and saith unto him, Rabbi, thou art the Son of God; thou art the King of Israel.   (John 1:45–49)

But Thomas, one of the twelve, called Didymus, was not with them when Jesus came. The other disciples therefore said unto him, We have seen the Lord. But he said unto them, Except I shall see in his hands the print of the nails, and put my finger into the print of the nails, and thrust my hand into his side, I will not believe. And after eight days again his disciples were within, and Thomas with them: then came Jesus, the doors being shut, and stood in the midst, and said, Peace be unto you. Then saith he to Thomas, Reach hither thy finger, and behold my hands; and reach hither thy hand, and thrust it into my side: and be not faithless, but believing. And Thomas answered and said unto him, My Lord and my God. Jesus saith unto him, Thomas, because thou hast seen me, thou hast believed: blessed are they that have not seen, and yet have believed. (John 20:24–29)

The officers answered, Never man spake like this man. (John 7:46)

Have I been so long time with you, and yet hast thou not known me, Philip? He that hath seen me hath seen the Father; and how sayest thou then, Show us the Father? Believest thou not that I am in the Father, and the Father in me? The words that I speak unto you I speak not of myself: but the Father that dwelleth in me, he doeth the works. Believe me that I am in the Father, and the Father in me: or else believe for the very works' sake. (John 14:9–11)

If I had not done among them the works which none other man did, they had not had sin: but now have they both seen and hated both me and my Father. (John 15:24)

He that is of God heareth God's words: ye therefore hear them not, because ye are not of God. (John 8:47)

For God sent not his Son into the world to condemn the world; but that the world through him might be saved. He that believeth on him is not condemned: but he that believeth not is condemned already, because he hath not believed in the name of the only begotten Son of God. And this is the condemnation, that light is come into the world, and men loved darkness rather than light, because their deeds were evil. For every one that doeth evil hateth the light, neither cometh to the light, lest his deeds should be reproved. But he that doeth truth cometh to the light, that his deeds may be made manifest, that they are wrought in God. (John 3:17–21)

And many other signs truly did Jesus in the presence of his disciples, which are not written in this book: but these are written, that ye might believe that Jesus is the Christ, the Son of God; and that believing ye might have life through his name. (John 20:30–31)

3. I DO NOT BELIEVE THERE IS A GOD.

That which may be known of God is manifest in them; for God hath showed it unto them. For the invisible things of him from the creation of the world are clearly seen, being understood by the things that are made, even his eternal power and Godhead; so that they are without excuse: because that, when they knew God, they glorified him not as God, neither were thankful; but became vain in their imaginations, and their foolish heart was darkened. Professing themselves to be wise, they became fools. (Romans 1:19–22)

The heavens declare the glory of God; and the firmament showeth his handiwork.   (Psalm 19:1)

The fool hath said in his heart, There is no God. They are corrupt, they have done abominable works, there is none that doeth good.   (Psalm 14:1)

4. IS THE BIBLE THE WORD OF GOD?

[You make] the word of God of none effect through your tradition, which ye have delivered: and many such like things do ye.   (Mark 7:13)

Heaven and earth shall pass away, but my words shall not pass away.   (Matthew 24:35)

Till heaven and earth pass, one jot or one tittle shall in no wise pass from the law, till all be fulfilled.   (Matthew 5:18)

Beginning at Moses and all the prophets, he expounded unto them in all the scriptures the things concerning himself. …And he said unto them, These are the words which I spake unto you, while I was yet with you, that all things must be fulfilled, which were written in the law of Moses, and in the prophets, and in the psalms, concerning me.   (Luke 24:27, 44)

For this cause also thank we God without ceasing, because, when ye received the word of God which ye heard of us, ye received it not as the word of men, but as it is in truth, the word of God, which effectually worketh also in you that believe.   (1 Thessalonians 2:13)

We have also a more sure word of prophecy; whereunto ye do well that ye take heed, as unto a light that shineth in a dark place, until the day dawn, and the day star arise in your hearts: knowing this first, that no prophecy of the scripture is of any private interpretation. For the prophecy came not in old time by the will of man: but holy men of God spake as they were moved by the Holy Ghost.   (2 Peter 1:19–21)

He that believeth on the Son of God hath the witness in himself: he that believeth not God hath made him a liar; because he believeth not the record that God gave of his Son. (1 John 5:10)

He that is of God heareth God's words: ye therefore hear them not, because ye are not of God. (John 8:47)

5. IS JESUS THE SON OF GOD?

The word which God sent unto the children of Israel, preaching peace by Jesus Christ: (he is Lord of all:) that word, I say, ye know. (Acts 10:36–37)

But we speak the wisdom of God in a mystery, even the hidden wisdom, which God ordained before the world unto our glory: which none of the princes of this world knew: for had they known it, they would not have crucified the Lord of glory. (1 Corinthians 2:7–8)

But unto the Son he saith, Thy throne, O God, is for ever and ever: a sceptre of righteousness is the sceptre of thy kingdom. (Hebrews 1:8)

And Thomas answered and said unto him, My Lord and my God. Jesus saith unto him, Thomas, because thou hast seen me, thou hast believed: blessed are they that have not seen, and yet have believed. (John 20:28–29)

But these are written, that ye might believe that Jesus is the Christ, the Son of God; and that believing ye might have life through his name. (John 20:31)

All men should honour the Son, even as they honour the Father. He that honoureth not the Son honoureth not the Father which hath sent him. (John 5:23)

Wherefore God also hath highly exalted him, and given him a name which is above every name: that at the name of Jesus every knee should bow, of things in heaven, and things in earth, and things under the earth. (Philippians 2:9–10)

Who is a liar but he that denieth that Jesus is the Christ? He is anti-christ, that denieth the Father and the Son. Whosoever denieth the Son, the same hath not the Father: (but) he that acknowledgeth the Son hath the Father also.   (1 John 2:22–23)

Whosoever believeth that Jesus is the Christ is born of God: and every one that loveth him that begat loveth him also that is begotten of him....Who is he that overcometh the world, but he that believeth that Jesus is the Son of God?   (1 John 5:1, 5)

Ye shall die in your sins: for if ye believe not that I am he, ye shall die in your sins.   (John 8:24)

CHAPTER 8

DEALING WITH OBJECTIONS

1. GOD IS UNJUST AND CRUEL TO CREATE MEN AND THEN DAMN THEM.

Nay but, O man, who art thou that repliest against God? Shall the thing formed say to him that formed it, Why hast thou made me thus? (Romans 9:20)

For my thoughts are not your thoughts, neither are your ways my ways, saith the LORD. For as the heavens are higher than the earth, so are my ways higher than your ways, and my thoughts than your thoughts. (Isaiah 55:8–9)

Shall he that contendeth with the Almighty instruct him? He that reproveth God, let him answer it. (Job 40:2)

My son, despise not thou the chastening of the Lord, nor faint when thou art rebuked of him: for whom the Lord loveth he chasteneth, and scourgeth every son whom he receiveth. …Now no chastening for the present seemeth to be joyous, but grievous: nevertheless afterward it yieldeth the peaceable fruit of righteousness unto them which are exercised thereby. (Hebrews 12:5–6, 11)

2. THE BIBLE HAS TOO MANY CONTRADICTIONS, AND I CANNOT UNDERSTAND IT.

But the natural man receiveth not the things of the Spirit of God: for they are foolishness unto him: neither can he know them, because they are spiritually discerned. (1 Corinthians 2:14)

*O the depth of the riches both of the wisdom and knowledge of God!
How unsearchable are his judgments, and his ways past finding out!*
(Romans 11:33)

*When I was a child, I spake as a child, I understood as a child, I
thought as a child: but when I became a man, I put away childish
things. For now we see through a glass, darkly; but then face to face:
now I know in part; but then shall I know even as also I am known.*
(1 Corinthians 13:11–12)

*Open thou mine eyes, that I may behold wondrous things out of thy
law.*   (Psalm 119:18)

*In all his epistles, [Paul spoke] in them of these things; in which are
some things hard to be understood, which they that are unlearned and
unstable wrest, as they do also the other scriptures, unto their own
destruction. Ye therefore, beloved, seeing ye know these things before,
beware lest ye also, being led away with the error of the wicked, fall
from your own stedfastness. But grow in grace, and in the knowledge
of our Lord and Saviour Jesus Christ. To him be glory both now and
for ever. Amen.*   (2 Peter 3:16–18)

3. THERE ARE TOO MANY HYPOCRITES IN CHURCH.

So then every one of us shall give account of himself to God.
(Romans 14:12)

*Therefore thou art inexcusable, O man, whosoever thou art that judg-
est: for wherein thou judgest another, thou condemnest thyself; for
thou that judgest doest the same things. But we are sure that the judgment of God is according to truth against them which commit such
things. And thinkest thou this, O man, that judgest them which do
such things, and doest the same, that thou shalt escape the judgment
of God? Or despisest thou the riches of his goodness and forbearance
and longsuffering; not knowing that the goodness of God leadeth thee
to repentance? But after thy hardness and impenitent heart treasurest*

up unto thyself wrath against the day of wrath and revelation of the righteous judgment of God.   (Romans 2:1–5)

Judge not, that ye be not judged. For with what judgment ye judge, ye shall be judged; and with what measure ye mete, it shall be measured to you again. And why beholdest thou the mote that is in thy brother's eye, but considerest not the beam that is in thine own eye? Or how wilt thou say to thy brother, Let me pull out the mote out of thine eye; and, behold, a beam is in thine own eye? Thou hypocrite, first cast out the beam out of thine own eye; and then shalt thou see clearly to cast out the mote out of thy brother's eye.   (Matthew 7:1–5)

4. I WILL ACCEPT CHRIST SOME TIME IN THE FUTURE.

Seek ye the LORD while he may be found, call ye upon him while he is near.   (Isaiah 55:6)

Boast not thyself of to morrow; for thou knowest not what a day may bring forth.   (Proverbs 27:1)

He, that being often reproved hardeneth his neck, shall suddenly be destroyed, and that without remedy.   (Proverbs 29:1)

Therefore be ye also ready: for in such an hour as ye think not the Son of man cometh.   (Matthew 24:44)

And while they went to buy, the bridegroom came; and they that were ready went in with him to the marriage: and the door was shut. Afterward came also the other virgins, saying, Lord, Lord, open to us. But he answered and said, Verily I say unto you, I know you not. Watch therefore, for ye know neither the day nor the hour wherein the Son of man cometh.   (Matthew 25:10–13)

And I will say to my soul, Soul, thou hast much goods laid up for many years; take thine ease, eat, drink, and be merry. But God said unto him, Thou fool, this night thy soul shall be required of thee: then

whose shall those things be, which thou hast provided?
(Luke 12:19–20)

*And Elijah came unto all the people, and said, How long halt ye
between two opinions? If the LORD be God, follow him: but if Baal,
then follow him.*   (1 Kings 18:21)

*Go to now, ye that say, To day or to morrow we will go into such
a city, and continue there a year, and buy and sell, and get gain:
whereas ye know not what shall be on the morrow. For what is your
life? It is even a vapour, that appeareth for a little time, and then
vanisheth away.*   (James 4:13–14)

*Strive to enter in at the strait gate: for many, I say unto you, will seek
to enter in, and shall not be able. When once the master of the house
is risen up, and hath shut to the door, and ye begin to stand without,
and to knock at the door, saying, Lord, Lord, open unto us; and he
shall answer and say unto you, I know you not whence ye are.*
(Luke 13:24–25)

*Yet a little while is the light with you. Walk while ye have the light,
lest darkness come upon you: for he that walketh in darkness knoweth
not whither he goeth.*   (John 12:35)

*But seek ye first the kingdom of God, and his righteousness; and all
these things shall be added unto you.*   (Matthew 6:33)

*Behold, now is the accepted time; behold, now is the day of salva-
tion.*   (2 Corinthians 6:2)

To day if ye will hear his voice, harden not your hearts.
(Hebrews 3:15)

*Remember now thy Creator in the days of thy youth, while the evil
days come not, nor the years draw nigh, when thou shalt say, I have
no pleasure in them.*   (Ecclesiastes 12:1)

He that is not with me is against me; and he that gathereth not with me scattereth abroad.   (Matthew 12:30)

5. I DO NOT WANT YOU TO TALK TO ME ABOUT CHRIST.

He that despised Moses' law died without mercy under two or three witnesses: of how much sorer punishment, suppose ye, shall he be thought worthy, who hath trodden under foot the Son of God, and hath counted the blood of the covenant, wherewith he was sanctified, an unholy thing, and hath done despite unto the Spirit of grace?
(Hebrews 10:28–29)

See that ye refuse not him that speaketh. For if they escaped not who refused him that spake on earth, much more shall not we escape, if we turn away from him that speaketh from heaven.   (Hebrews 12:25)

He that believeth and is baptized shall be saved; but he that believeth not shall be damned.   (Mark 16:16)

For that they hated knowledge, and did not choose the fear of the LORD: *they would none of my counsel: they despised all my reproof. Therefore shall they eat of the fruit of their own way, and be filled with their own devices. For the turning away of the simple shall slay them, and the prosperity of fools shall destroy them. But whoso hearkeneth unto me shall dwell safely, and shall be quiet from fear of evil.*
(Proverbs 1:29–33)

6. THERE IS SOMEONE I CANNOT FORGIVE.

But if ye forgive not men their trespasses, neither will your Father forgive your trespasses.   (Matthew 6:15)

Therefore is the kingdom of heaven likened unto a certain king, which would take account of his servants. And when he had begun to reckon, one was brought unto him, which owed him ten thousand talents. But forasmuch as he had not to pay, his lord commanded him to be sold, and his wife, and children, and all that he had, and payment to be made. The servant therefore fell down, and worshipped him, saying, Lord, have patience with me, and I will pay thee all. Then the lord of that servant was moved with compassion, and loosed him, and forgave him the debt. But the same servant went out, and found one of his fellowservants, which owed him an hundred pence: and he laid hands on him, and took him by the throat, saying, Pay me that thou owest. And his fellowservant fell down at his feet, and besought him, saying, Have patience with me, and I will pay thee all. And he would not: but went and cast him into prison, till he should pay the debt. So when his fellowservants saw what was done, they were very sorry, and came and told unto their lord all that was done. Then his lord, after that he had called him, said unto him, O thou wicked servant, I forgave thee all that debt, because thou desiredst me: shouldest not thou also have had compassion on thy fellowservant, even as I had pity on thee? And his lord was wroth, and delivered him to the tormentors, till he should pay all that was due unto him. So likewise shall my heavenly Father do also unto you, if ye from your hearts forgive not every one his brother their trespasses.   (Matthew 18:23–35)

And be ye kind one to another, tenderhearted, forgiving one another, even as God for Christ's sake hath forgiven you.   (Ephesians 4:32)

I can do all things through Christ which strengtheneth me.
                                                    (Philippians 4:13)

CHAPTER 9

SPECIAL TEXTS FOR SPECIAL PEOPLE

1. I AM A ROMAN CATHOLIC.

Jesus answered and said unto him, Verily, verily, I say unto thee, Except a man be born again, he cannot see the kingdom of God. ... Verily, verily, I say unto thee, Except a man be born of water and of the Spirit, he cannot enter into the kingdom of God. ...Marvel not that I said unto thee, Ye must be born again.   (John 3:3, 5, 7)

Whosoever is born of God doth not commit sin; for his seed remaineth in him: and he cannot sin, because he is born of God. ...We know that we have passed from death unto life, because we love the brethren. He that loveth not his brother abideth in death. Whosoever hateth his brother is a murderer: and ye know that no murderer hath eternal life abiding in him. Hereby perceive we the love of God, because he laid down his life for us: and we ought to lay down our lives for the brethren. But whoso hath this world's good, and seeth his brother have need, and shutteth up his bowels of compassion from him, how dwelleth the love of God in him?   (1 John 3:9, 14–17)

But to him that worketh not, but believeth on him that justifieth the ungodly, his faith is counted for righteousness.   (Romans 4:5)

For there is one God, and one mediator between God and men, the man Christ Jesus.   (1 Timothy 2:5)

I acknowledged my sin unto thee, and mine iniquity have I not hid. I said, I will confess my transgressions unto the LORD; and thou forgavest the iniquity of my sin.   (Psalm 32:5)

These things have I written unto you that believe on the name of the Son of God; that ye may know that ye have eternal life.

(1 John 5:13)

And by him all that believe are justified from all things, from which ye could not be justified by the law of Moses.   (Acts 13:39)

Search the scriptures; for in them ye think ye have eternal life: and they are they which testify of me.   (John 5:39)

Wherefore laying aside all malice, and all guile, and hypocrisies, and envies, and all evil speakings, as newborn babes, desire the sincere milk of the word, that ye may grow thereby.   (1 Peter 2:1–2)

But evil men and seducers shall wax worse and worse, deceiving, and being deceived. But continue thou in the things which thou hast learned and hast been assured of, knowing of whom thou hast learned them; and that from a child thou hast known the holy scriptures, which are able to make thee wise unto salvation through faith which is in Christ Jesus. All scripture is given by inspiration of God, and is profitable for doctrine, for reproof, for correction, for instruction in righteousness: that the man of God may be perfect, thoroughly furnished unto all good works.   (2 Timothy 3:13–17)

Howbeit in vain do they worship me, teaching for doctrines the commandments of men. For laying aside the commandment of God, ye hold the tradition of men, as the washing of pots and cups: and many other such like things ye do…making the word of God of none effect through your tradition, which ye have delivered: and many such like things do ye.   (Mark 7:7–8, 13)

Ye do err, not knowing the scriptures, nor the power of God.

(Matthew 22:29)

2. I AM A JEW.

Who hath believed our report? And to whom is the arm of the LORD revealed? For he shall grow up before him as a tender plant, and as a root out of a dry ground: he hath no form nor comeliness; and when we shall see him, there is no beauty that we should desire him. He is despised and rejected of men; a man of sorrows, and acquainted with grief: and we hid as it were our faces from him; he was despised, and we esteemed him not. Surely he hath borne our griefs, and carried our sorrows: yet we did esteem him stricken, smitten of God, and afflicted. But he was wounded for our transgressions, he was bruised for our iniquities: the chastisement of our peace was upon him; and with his stripes we are healed. All we like sheep have gone astray; we have turned every one to his own way; and the LORD *hath laid on him the iniquity of us all. He was oppressed, and he was afflicted, yet he opened not his mouth: he is brought as a lamb to the slaughter, and as a sheep before her shearers is dumb, so he openeth not his mouth. He was taken from prison and from judgment: and who shall declare his generation? For he was cut off out of the land of the living: for the transgression of my people was he stricken. And he made his grave with the wicked, and with the rich in his death; because he had done no violence, neither was any deceit in his mouth. Yet it pleased the* LORD *to bruise him; he hath put him to grief: when thou shalt make his soul an offering for sin, he shall see his seed, he shall prolong his days, and the pleasure of the* LORD *shall prosper in his hand. He shall see of the travail of his soul, and shall be satisfied: by his knowledge shall my righteous servant justify many; for he shall bear their iniquities. Therefore will I divide him a portion with the great, and he shall divide the spoil with the strong; because he hath poured out his soul unto death: and he was numbered with the transgressors; and he bare the sin of many, and made intercession for the transgressors.*

(Isaiah 53)

And I will pour upon the house of David, and upon the inhabitants of Jerusalem, the spirit of grace and of supplications: and they shall look upon me whom they have pierced, and they shall mourn for him, as one mourneth for his only son, and shall be in bitterness for him, as one that is in bitterness for his firstborn.   (Zechariah 12:10)

And after threescore and two weeks shall Messiah be cut off, but not for himself: and the people of the prince that shall come shall destroy the city and the sanctuary; and the end thereof shall be with a flood, and unto the end of the war desolations are determined.

(Daniel 9:26)

3. I AM A SPIRITUALIST.

And when they shall say unto you, Seek unto them that have familiar spirits, and unto wizards that peep, and that mutter: should not a people seek unto their God? for the living to the dead? To the law and to the testimony: if they speak not according to this word, it is because there is no light in them. (Isaiah 8:19–20)

Beloved, believe not every spirit, but try the spirits whether they are of God: because many false prophets are gone out into the world. Hereby know ye the Spirit of God: Every spirit that confesseth that Jesus Christ is come in the flesh is of God: and every spirit that confesseth not that Jesus Christ is come in the flesh is not of God: and this is that spirit of antichrist, whereof ye have heard that it should come; and even now already is it in the world. (1 John 4:1–3)

Regard not them that have familiar spirits, neither seek after wizards, to be defiled by them: I am the Lord *your God.* (Leviticus 19:31)

And the soul that turneth after such as have familiar spirits, and after wizards, to go a whoring after them, I will even set my face against that soul, and will cut him off from among his people.

(Leviticus 20:6)

There shall not be found among you any one that maketh his son or his daughter to pass through the fire, or that useth divination, or an observer of times, or an enchanter, or a witch, or a charmer, or a consulter with familiar spirits, or a wizard, or a necromancer. For all that do these things are an abomination unto the Lord*: and because of these abominations the* Lord *thy God doth drive them out from before thee.* (Deuteronomy 18:10–12)

Then shall that Wicked be revealed...even him, whose coming is after the working of Satan with all power and signs and lying wonders, and with all deceivableness of unrighteousness in them that perish; because they received not the love of the truth, that they might be saved. And for this cause God shall send them strong delusion, that they should believe a lie: that they all might be damned who believed not the truth, but had pleasure in unrighteousness.

(2 Thessalonians 2:8–12)

So Saul died for his transgression which he committed against the Lord, *even against the word of the* Lord, *which he kept not, and also for asking counsel of one that had a familiar spirit, to inquire of it; and inquired not of the* Lord: *therefore he slew him, and turned the kingdom unto David the son of Jesse.*   (1 Chronicles 10:13–14)

CHAPTER 10

BECOMING A MATURE BELIEVER

1. CONFESSING CHRIST BEFORE THE WORLD

Whosoever therefore shall confess me before men, him will I confess also before my Father which is in heaven. But whosoever shall deny me before men, him will I also deny before my Father which is in heaven. (Matthew 10:32–33)

If thou shalt confess with thy mouth the Lord Jesus, and shalt believe in thine heart that God hath raised him from the dead, thou shalt be saved. For with the heart man believeth unto righteousness; and with the mouth confession is made unto salvation. (Romans 10:9–10)

Nevertheless among the chief rulers also many believed on him; but because of the Pharisees they did not confess him, lest they should be put out of the synagogue: for they loved the praise of men more than the praise of God. (John 12:42–43)

Whosoever therefore shall be ashamed of me and of my words in this adulterous and sinful generation; of him also shall the Son of man be ashamed, when he cometh in the glory of his Father with the holy angels. (Mark 8:38)

2. THE BIBLE—GOD'S MESSAGE TO MAN

As newborn babes, desire the sincere milk of the word, that ye may grow thereby. (1 Peter 2:2)

And now, brethren, I commend you to God, and to the word of his grace, which is able to build you up, and to give you an inheritance among all them which are sanctified. (Acts 20:32)

Wherefore lay apart all filthiness and superfluity of naughtiness, and receive with meekness the engrafted word, which is able to save your souls. But be ye doers of the word, and not hearers only, deceiving your own selves. (James 1:21–22)

All scripture is given by inspiration of God, and is profitable for doctrine, for reproof, for correction, for instruction in righteousness: that the man of God may be perfect, thoroughly furnished unto all good works. (2 Timothy 3:16–17)

And take the helmet of salvation, and the sword of the Spirit, which is the word of God. (Ephesians 6:17)

Wherewithal shall a young man cleanse his way? By taking heed thereto according to thy word. …Thy word have I hid in mine heart, that I might not sin against thee.…The entrance of thy words giveth light; it giveth understanding unto the simple. (Psalm 119:9, 11, 130)

Blessed is the man that walketh not in the counsel of the ungodly, nor standeth in the way of sinners, nor sitteth in the seat of the scornful. But his delight is in the law of the LORD; and in his law doth he meditate day and night. (Psalm 1:1–2)

This book of the law shall not depart out of thy mouth; but thou shalt meditate therein day and night, that thou mayest observe to do according to all that is written therein: for then thou shalt make thy way prosperous, and then thou shalt have good success. (Joshua 1:8)

These were more noble than those in Thessalonica, in that they received the word with all readiness of mind, and searched the scriptures daily, whether those things were so. (Acts 17:11)

3. THE PRIVILEGE OF PRAYER

Ye lust, and have not: ye kill, and desire to have, and cannot obtain: ye fight and war, yet ye have not, because ye ask not. (James 4:2)

Ask, and it shall be given you; seek, and ye shall find; knock, and it shall be opened unto you. For every one that asketh receiveth; and he that seeketh findeth; and to him that knocketh it shall be opened. If a son shall ask bread of any of you that is a father, will he give him a stone? Or if he ask a fish, will he for a fish give him a serpent? Or if he shall ask an egg, will he offer him a scorpion? If ye then, being evil, know how to give good gifts unto your children: how much more shall your heavenly Father give the Holy Spirit to them that ask him?

(Luke 11:9–13)

Is any among you afflicted? Let him pray. Is any merry? let him sing psalms. Is any sick among you? Let him call for the elders of the church; and let them pray over him, anointing him with oil in the name of the Lord: and the prayer of faith shall save the sick, and the Lord shall raise him up; and if he have committed sins, they shall be forgiven him. Confess your faults one to another, and pray one for another, that ye may be healed. The effectual fervent prayer of a righteous man availeth much. Elias was a man subject to like passions as we are, and he prayed earnestly that it might not rain: and it rained not on the earth by the space of three years and six months. And he prayed again, and the heaven gave rain, and the earth brought forth her fruit.

(James 5:13–18)

Why sleep ye? rise and pray, lest ye enter into temptation.

(Luke 22:46)

But they that wait upon the LORD shall renew their strength; they shall mount up with wings as eagles; they shall run, and not be weary; and they shall walk, and not faint.

(Isaiah 40:31)

Evening, and morning, and at noon, will I pray, and cry aloud: and he shall hear my voice.

(Psalm 55:17)

Now when Daniel knew that the writing was signed, he went into his house; and his windows being open in his chamber toward Jerusalem, he kneeled upon his knees three times a day, and prayed, and gave thanks before his God, as he did aforetime.

(Daniel 6:10)

And when [Jesus] had sent them away, he departed into a mountain to pray. (Mark 6:46)

And it came to pass in those days, that [Jesus] went out into a mountain to pray, and continued all night in prayer to God. (Luke 6:12)

Pray without ceasing. (1 Thessalonians 5:17)

4. LIVING A HOLY LIFE

Be ye not unequally yoked together with unbelievers: for what fellowship hath righteousness with unrighteousness? And what communion hath light with darkness? And what concord hath Christ with Belial? Or what part hath he that believeth with an infidel? And what agreement hath the temple of God with idols? For ye are the temple of the living God; as God hath said, I will dwell in them, and walk in them; and I will be their God, and they shall be my people. Wherefore come out from among them, and be ye separate, saith the Lord, and touch not the unclean thing; and I will receive you, and will be a Father unto you, and ye shall be my sons and daughters, saith the Lord Almighty. Having therefore these promises, dearly beloved, let us cleanse ourselves from all filthiness of the flesh and spirit, perfecting holiness in the fear of God. (2 Corinthians 6:14–7:1)

No man can serve two masters: for either he will hate the one, and love the other; or else he will hold to the one, and despise the other. Ye cannot serve God and mammon. (Matthew 6:24)

Love not the world, neither the things that are in the world. If any man love the world, the love of the Father is not in him. For all that is in the world, the lust of the flesh, and the lust of the eyes, and the pride of life, is not of the Father, but is of the world. And the world passeth away, and the lust thereof: but he that doeth the will of God abideth for ever. (1 John 2:15–17)

Know ye not that the friendship of the world is enmity with God? Whosoever therefore will be a friend of the world is the enemy of

God. ...*But he giveth more grace. Wherefore he saith, God resisteth the proud, but giveth grace unto the humble. Submit yourselves therefore to God. Resist the devil, and he will flee from you. Draw nigh to God, and he will draw nigh to you. Cleanse your hands, ye sinners; and purify your hearts, ye double minded.*   (James 4:4, 6–8)

Follow peace with all men, and holiness, without which no man shall see the Lord.   (Hebrews 12:14)

As obedient children, not fashioning yourselves according to the former lusts in your ignorance: but as he which hath called you is holy, so be ye holy in all manner of conversation; because it is written, Be ye holy; for I am holy. And if ye call on the Father, who without respect of persons judgeth according to every man's work, pass the time of your sojourning here in fear: forasmuch as ye know that ye were not redeemed with corruptible things, as silver and gold, from your vain conversation received by tradition from your fathers; but with the precious blood of Christ, as of a lamb without blemish and without spot.   (1 Peter 1:14–19)

For the time is come that judgment must begin at the house of God: and if it first begin at us, what shall the end be of them that obey not the gospel of God? And if the righteous scarcely be saved, where shall the ungodly and the sinner appear?   (1 Peter 4:17–18)

And that which fell among thorns are they, which, when they have heard, go forth, and are choked with cares and riches and pleasures of this life, and bring no fruit to perfection.   (Luke 8:14)

Take heed to yourselves, lest at any time your hearts be overcharged with surfeiting, and drunkenness, and cares of this life, and so that day come upon you unawares. For as a snare shall it come on all them that dwell on the face of the whole earth. Watch ye therefore, and pray always, that ye may be accounted worthy to escape all these things that shall come to pass, and to stand before the Son of man.   (Luke 21:34–36)

I beseech you therefore, brethren, by the mercies of God, that ye present your bodies a living sacrifice, holy, acceptable unto God, which is your reasonable service. And be not conformed to this world: but be ye transformed by the renewing of your mind, that ye may prove what is that good, and acceptable, and perfect, will of God.

(Romans 12:1–2)

I have fought a good fight, I have finished my course, I have kept the faith: henceforth there is laid up for me a crown of righteousness, which the Lord, the righteous judge, shall give me at that day: and not to me only, but unto all them also that love his appearing.

(2 Timothy 4:7–8)

5. WORKING FOR CHRIST

For the Son of man is as a man taking a far journey, who left his house, and gave authority to his servants, and to every man his work, and commanded the porter to watch. Watch ye therefore: for ye know not when the master of the house cometh, at even, or at midnight, or at the cockcrowing, or in the morning: lest coming suddenly he find you sleeping. And what I say unto you I say unto all, Watch.

(Mark 13:34–37)

Therefore be ye also ready: for in such an hour as ye think not the Son of man cometh. Who then is a faithful and wise servant, whom his lord hath made ruler over his household, to give them meat in due season? Blessed is that servant, whom his lord when he cometh shall find so doing. Verily I say unto you, That he shall make him ruler over all his goods. But and if that evil servant shall say in his heart, My lord delayeth his coming; and shall begin to smite his fellowservants, and to eat and drink with the drunken; the lord of that servant shall come in a day when he looketh not for him, and in an hour that he is not aware of, and shall cut him asunder, and appoint him his portion with the hypocrites: there shall be weeping and gnashing of teeth.
(Matthew 24:44–51)

For the kingdom of heaven is as a man travelling into a far country, who called his own servants, and delivered unto them his goods. And unto one he gave five talents, to another two, and to another one; to every man according to his several ability; and straightway took his journey. Then he that had received the five talents went and traded with the same, and made them other five talents. And likewise he that had received two, he also gained other two. But he that had received one went and digged in the earth, and hid his lord's money. After a long time the lord of those servants cometh, and reckoneth with them. And so he that had received five talents came and brought other five talents, saying, Lord, thou deliveredst unto me five talents: behold, I have gained beside them five talents more. His lord said unto him, Well done, thou good and faithful servant: thou hast been faithful over a few things, I will make thee ruler over many things: enter thou into the joy of thy lord. He also that had received two talents came and said, Lord, thou deliveredst unto me two talents: behold, I have gained two other talents beside them. His lord said unto him, Well done, good and faithful servant; thou hast been faithful over a few things, I will make thee ruler over many things: enter thou into the joy of thy lord. Then he which had received the one talent came and said, Lord, I knew thee that thou art an hard man, reaping where thou hast not sown, and gathering where thou hast not strowed: and I was afraid, and went and hid thy talent in the earth: lo, there thou hast that is thine. His lord answered and said unto him, Thou wicked and slothful servant, thou knewest that I reap where I sowed not, and gather where I have not strowed: thou oughtest therefore to have put my money to the exchangers, and then at my coming I should have received mine own with usury. Take therefore the talent from him, and give it unto him which hath ten talents. For unto every one that hath shall be given, and he shall have abundance: but from him that hath not shall be taken away even that which he hath. And cast ye the unprofitable servant into outer darkness: there shall be weeping and gnashing of teeth.   (Matthew 25:14–30)

Therefore they that were scattered abroad went every where preaching the word.   (Acts 8:4)

That we henceforth be no more children, tossed to and fro, and carried about with every wind of doctrine, by the sleight of men, and cunning craftiness, whereby they lie in wait to deceive; but speaking the truth in love, may grow up into him in all things, which is the head, even Christ: from whom the whole body fitly joined together and compacted by that which every joint supplieth, according to the effectual working in the measure of every part, maketh increase of the body unto the edifying of itself in love. (Ephesians 4:14–16)

Awake thou that sleepest, and arise from the dead, and Christ shall give thee light. See then that ye walk circumspectly, not as fools, but as wise, redeeming the time, because the days are evil. Wherefore be ye not unwise, but understanding what the will of the Lord is. And be not drunk with wine, wherein is excess; but be filled with the Spirit; speaking to yourselves in psalms and hymns and spiritual songs, singing and making melody in your heart to the Lord; giving thanks always for all things unto God and the Father in the name of our Lord Jesus Christ; submitting yourselves one to another in the fear of God. (Ephesians 5:14–21)

Let him know, that he which converteth the sinner from the error of his way shall save a soul from death, and shall hide a multitude of sins. (James 5:20)

And they that be wise shall shine as the brightness of the firmament; and they that turn many to righteousness as the stars for ever and ever. (Daniel 12:3)

And, behold, I come quickly; and my reward is with me, to give every man according as his work shall be. (Revelation 22:12)

CHAPTER 11

STRENGTH FOR DIFFICULT TIMES

1. VICTORY OVER TEMPTATION

My brethren, count it all joy when ye fall into divers temptations; knowing this, that the trying of your faith worketh patience. But let patience have her perfect work, that ye may be perfect and entire, wanting nothing. (James 1:2–4)

Blessed is the man that endureth temptation: for when he is tried, he shall receive the crown of life, which the Lord hath promised to them that love him. (James 1:12)

Be sober, be vigilant; because your adversary the devil, as a roaring lion, walketh about, seeking whom he may devour: whom resist stedfast in the faith, knowing that the same afflictions are accomplished in your brethren that are in the world. But the God of all grace, who hath called us unto his eternal glory by Christ Jesus, after that ye have suffered a while, make you perfect, stablish, strengthen, settle you. (1 Peter 5:8–10)

There hath no temptation taken you but such as is common to man: but God is faithful, who will not suffer you to be tempted above that ye are able; but will with the temptation also make a way to escape, that ye may be able to bear it. (1 Corinthians 10:13)

And he said unto me, My grace is sufficient for thee: for my strength is made perfect in weakness. Most gladly therefore will I rather glory in my infirmities, that the power of Christ may rest upon me. Therefore I take pleasure in infirmities, in reproaches, in necessities,

*in persecutions, in distresses for Christ's sake: for when I am weak,
then am I strong.* (2 Corinthians 12:9–10)

Pray without ceasing. (1 Thessalonians 5:17)

*Every spirit that confesseth not that Jesus Christ is come in the flesh is
not of God.... Ye are of God, little children, and have overcome them:
because greater is he that is in you, than he that is in the world.*
(1 John 4:3–4)

I can do all things through Christ which strengtheneth me.
(Philippians 4:13)

*I have written unto you, fathers, because ye have known him that is
from the beginning. I have written unto you, young men, because ye
are strong, and the word of God abideth in you, and ye have overcome
the wicked one.* (1 John 2:14)

*Wherewithal shall a young man cleanse his way? By taking heed
thereto according to thy word.* (Psalm 119:9)

2. REJOICING IN PERSECUTION

*Blessed are they which are persecuted for righteousness' sake: for theirs
is the kingdom of heaven. Blessed are ye, when men shall revile you,
and persecute you, and shall say all manner of evil against you falsely,
for my sake. Rejoice, and be exceeding glad: for great is your reward
in heaven: for so persecuted they the prophets which were before you.*
(Matthew 5:10–12)

*Beloved, think it not strange concerning the fiery trial which is to try
you, as though some strange thing happened unto you: but rejoice,
inasmuch as ye are partakers of Christ's sufferings; that, when his
glory shall be revealed, ye may be glad also with exceeding joy. If ye be
reproached for the name of Christ, happy are ye; for the spirit of glory
and of God resteth upon you: on their part he is evil spoken of, but on
your part he is glorified.* (1 Peter 4:12–14)

If any man suffer as a Christian, let him not be ashamed; but let him glorify God on this behalf.   (1 Peter 4:16)

For even hereunto were ye called: because Christ also suffered for us, leaving us an example, that ye should follow his steps...who, when he was reviled, reviled not again; when he suffered, he threatened not; but committed himself to him that judgeth righteously.
                                                    (1 Peter 2:21, 23)

For it is better, if the will of God be so, that ye suffer for well doing, than for evil doing. For Christ also hath once suffered for sins, the just for the unjust, that he might bring us to God, being put to death in the flesh, but quickened by the Spirit.   (1 Peter 3:17–18)

Yea, and all that will live godly in Christ Jesus shall suffer persecution.   (2 Timothy 3:12)

If we suffer, we shall also reign with him: if we deny him, he also will deny us.   (2 Timothy 2:12)

Continue in the faith...[for] we must through much tribulation enter into the kingdom of God.   (Acts 14:22)

And when they had called the apostles, and beaten them, they commanded that they should not speak in the name of Jesus, and let them go. And they departed from the presence of the council, rejoicing that they were counted worthy to suffer shame for his name. And daily in the temple, and in every house, they ceased not to teach and preach Jesus Christ.   (Acts 5:40–42)

Wherefore seeing we also are compassed about with so great a cloud of witnesses, let us lay aside every weight, and the sin which doth so easily beset us, and let us run with patience the race that is set before us, looking unto Jesus the author and finisher of our faith; who for the joy that was set before him endured the cross, despising the shame, and is set down at the right hand of the throne of God. For consider him that endured such contradiction of sinners against himself, lest ye be wearied and faint in your minds. Ye have not yet resisted unto blood, striving against sin.　　　　　　　(Hebrews 12:1–4)

Fear none of those things which thou shalt suffer: behold, the devil shall cast some of you into prison, that ye may be tried; and ye shall have tribulation ten days: be thou faithful unto death, and I will give thee a crown of life.　　　　　　　(Revelation 2:10)

3. PERSEVERING THROUGH TRIAL

An inheritance incorruptible, and undefiled, and that fadeth not away [is] *reserved in heaven for you, who are kept by the power of God through faith unto salvation ready to be revealed in the last time. Wherein ye greatly rejoice, though now for a season, if need be, ye are in heaviness through manifold temptations: that the trial of your faith, being much more precious than of gold that perisheth, though it be tried with fire, might be found unto praise and honour and glory at the appearing of Jesus Christ.*　　　　　　　(1 Peter 1:4–7)

Humble yourselves therefore under the mighty hand of God, that he may exalt you in due time: casting all your care upon him; for he careth for you.　　　　　　　(1 Peter 5:6–7)

God is our refuge and strength, a very present help in trouble. Therefore will not we fear, though the earth be removed, and though the mountains be carried into the midst of the sea; though the waters thereof roar and be troubled, though the mountains shake with the swelling thereof.　　　　　　　(Psalm 46:1–3)

Yea, though I walk through the valley of the shadow of death, I will fear no evil: for thou art with me; thy rod and thy staff they comfort me.　　　　　　　(Psalm 23:4)

Many are the afflictions of the righteous: but the Lord *delivereth him out of them all.*　　　　　　　(Psalm 34:19)

Call upon me in the day of trouble: I will deliver thee, and thou shalt glorify me.　　　　　　　(Psalm 50:15)

The righteous cry, and the LORD *heareth, and delivereth them out of all their troubles.* (Psalm 34:17)

The LORD *is my light and my salvation; whom shall I fear? The* LORD *is the strength of my life; of whom shall I be afraid? When the wicked, even mine enemies and my foes, came upon me to eat up my flesh, they stumbled and fell. Though an host should encamp against me, my heart shall not fear: though war should rise against me, in this will I be confident. One thing have I desired of the* LORD, *that will I seek after; that I may dwell in the house of the* LORD *all the days of my life, to behold the beauty of the* LORD, *and to inquire in his temple. For in the time of trouble he shall hide me in his pavilion: in the secret of his tabernacle shall he hide me; he shall set me up upon a rock. And now shall mine head be lifted up above mine enemies round about me: therefore will I offer in his tabernacle sacrifices of joy; I will sing, yea, I will sing praises unto the* LORD. *...I had fainted, unless I had believed to see the goodness of the* LORD *in the land of the living. Wait on the* LORD: *be of good courage, and he shall strengthen thine heart: wait, I say, on the* LORD. (Psalm 27:1–6, 13–14)

Come unto me, all ye that labour and are heavy laden, and I will give you rest. Take my yoke upon you, and learn of me; for I am meek and lowly in heart: and ye shall find rest unto your souls.
(Matthew 11:28–29)

4. COMFORT IN TIME OF LOSS

Let not your heart be troubled: ye believe in God, believe also in me. In my Father's house are many mansions: if it were not so, I would have told you. I go to prepare a place for you. And if I go and prepare a place for you, I will come again, and receive you unto myself; that where I am, there ye may be also. ...Peace I leave with you, my peace I give unto you: not as the world giveth, give I unto you. Let not your heart be troubled, neither let it be afraid. (John 14:1–3, 27)

Be still, and know that I am God. (Psalm 46:10)

And I heard a voice from heaven saying unto me, Write, Blessed are the dead which die in the Lord from henceforth: Yea, saith the Spirit, that they may rest from their labours; and their works do follow them.   (Revelation 14:13)

But I would not have you to be ignorant, brethren, concerning them which are asleep, that ye sorrow not, even as others which have no hope. For if we believe that Jesus died and rose again, even so them also which sleep in Jesus will God bring with him. For this we say unto you by the word of the Lord, that we which are alive and remain unto the coming of the Lord shall not prevent them which are asleep. For the Lord himself shall descend from heaven with a shout, with the voice of the archangel, and with the trump of God: and the dead in Christ shall rise first: then we which are alive and remain shall be caught up together with them in the clouds, to meet the Lord in the air: and so shall we ever be with the Lord. Wherefore comfort one another with these words.   (1 Thessalonians 4:13–18)

Therefore we are always confident, knowing that, whilst we are at home in the body, we are absent from the Lord: (for we walk by faith, not by sight:) we are confident, I say, and willing rather to be absent from the body, and to be present with the Lord.
                                                      (2 Corinthians 5:6–8)

For I am in a strait betwixt two, having a desire to depart, and to be with Christ; which is far better.   (Philippians 1:23)

For this corruptible must put on incorruption, and this mortal must put on immortality. So when this corruptible shall have put on incorruption, and this mortal shall have put on immortality, then shall be brought to pass the saying that is written, Death is swallowed up in victory. O death, where is thy sting? O grave, where is thy victory? The sting of death is sin; and the strength of sin is the law. But thanks be to God, which giveth us the victory through our Lord Jesus Christ. Therefore, my beloved brethren, be ye stedfast, unmoveable, always abounding in the work of the Lord, forasmuch as ye know that your labour is not in vain in the Lord.   (1 Corinthians 15:53–58)

CHAPTER 12

HELPFUL SOULWINNING HINTS

1. Generally deal with people of your own sex and close to your own age.

2. Whenever it is possible, talk to the person alone.

3. Rely completely on the Spirit of God.

4. Do not merely quote or read passages from the Bible but have the one with whom you are speaking read them for himself.

5. Emphasize a single passage of Scripture, repeating and discussing it until the inquirer cannot forget it. He will hear it ringing in his memory long after you have ceased talking.

6. Always hold the person to the main point of accepting Christ. Many opportunities for repentance have been lost by an inexperienced worker allowing himself to become involved in an argument over some side issue.

7. Be courteous. Some overzealous workers cause the people they approach to become defensive and to put up barriers that are impossible to penetrate.

8. Be earnest. Genuine earnestness means more than any skill learned in a training class or even from a book such as this.

9. Never lose your temper.

10. Never interrupt anyone else who is leading someone to Christ.

11. Do not be in a hurry.

12. Ask the person to pray with you. Difficulties can disappear during prayer, and many stubborn people yield when they are brought into the presence of God.

13. Whenever you seem to fail, go home, pray about it, and find out why you failed. Then go back, if you can, and try again.

14. Be sure to give the new believer definite instructions concerning how to succeed in the Christian life.

15. Spend time with the new believer regularly to encourage him and to help him grow as a Christian.

ABOUT THE AUTHOR

Reuben Archer Torrey (1856–1928) is respected as one of the greatest evangelists of modern times. Several years after his graduation from Yale Divinity School, he was selected by D. L. Moody to become the first dean of the Moody Bible Institute of Chicago. Under his direction, Moody Institute became a pattern for Bible institutes around the world.

Dr. Torrey spent the years of 1903–1905 in worldwide revival campaigns, winning thousands of souls to Jesus Christ. He continued worldwide crusades for the next fifteen years while he served as the dean of the Bible Institute of Los Angeles and pastored the Church of the Open Door in that city.

Torrey longed for more Christian workers to take an active part in bringing the message of salvation through Christ to a lost and dying world. His straightforward style of evangelism has shown thousands of Christian workers how to become effective soulwinners.